# FOLKLORE OF SOUTHERN INDIA

First published 1890
This edition published by Lector House in 2023

ISBN: 978-93-5614-812-3


Lector House LLP
Registered Office: H. No. 96, Block C, Tomar Colony,
Burari, Delhi – 110084, India
info@lectorhouse.com
www.lectorhouse.com

# FOLKLORE OF SOUTHERN INDIA

PANDIT NATESA SASTRI,
MRS. HOWARD KINGSCOTE (LUCAS CLEEVE)

2023

LECTOR HOUSE

LECTOR HOUSE LLP

# FOLKLORE OF SOUTHERN INDIA;

## OR,

## TALES OF THE SUN

COLLECTED BY

PAṆḌIT NAṬÊSÁ SÁSTRÎ
AND
MRS. HOWARD KINGSCOTE

# PREFACE.

In offering these few Indian tales to the public, I cannot refrain from adding a few words at the beginning to express to Paṇḍit Natêśa Sástrî my gratitude for the great assistance he has given me in collecting them, assistance without which they would never have seen the light in the shape of a complete volume. When I began writing down these tales, my only means of collecting them was through my native servants, who used to get them from the old women in the bazaars; but the fables they brought me were as full of corruptions and foreign adaptions as the miscellaneous ingredients that find their way into a dish of their own curry and rice, and had it not been for Mr. Sástrî's timely aid, my small work would have gone forth to the world laden with inaccuracies.

Mr. Sástrî not only corrected the errors of my own tales, but allowed me to add to them many that he had himself collected, and that had already been published, either in small volumes or in numbers of *The Indian Antiquary*. For this reason I have left several notes which Mr. Cowper Temple, Mr. Clowston, and others had added to the tales that had already been printed, as they were too valuable to dispense with, and may be of service to students of folklore. In conclusion, I would crave the indulgence of my readers with regard to the style in which the tales are written, which has been left as nearly as possible in the form of a literal translation, in order to lend the Stories a "*couleur locale,*" which is characteristic of the country they spring from.

G. K.

# CONTENTS

# INTRODUCTION.

It has often struck all lovers of Folklore and National Legends with wonder, that so many countries should have reproduced in different imagery and language the same tales. Persia, Arabia, and India give us the same fables as Italy, France, Norway, and Iceland, except for slight variations principally arising from difference of custom, distance of time, idiom and nationality.

Able writers have explained this to us by a theory worthy of consideration, and admirable in its origin, but nevertheless wholly their own. They would have us believe that a certain group of tales belonged to a certain nation, and that through emigration and immigration, through wars and dispersions, these same tales have been carried backwards and forwards and dragged from country to country borrowing the language and peculiarities of the lands they passed through, just as the seed of some rare plant is borne on the breeze and bears fruit coarse or more refined according to the soil in which it at last takes root.

In Germany we have Gödeck, Köhler, Sichecht, and a host of others who tell us that these tales are Oriental, and that all fable originates in the East, others again that they are transmitted to us by the same channel as the Aryan languages from Aryan tradition. I cannot see why one nation or one country alone should have the intelligence of producing fables which as a rule are next to religion in their teaching and intentions. If proverbs are the wisdom of nations, what are fables and legends but developed proverbs. What is the meaning of fable? It means an intent to convey moral instruction in a narrative in which the characters are represented by birds, beasts, or fishes; and often plants.

Practically a parable is the same thing, and folklore and fairy-tales are the attempts of intelligent people to inculcate in their children or other ignorant people the great truths of religion or wisdom, by means of word-pictures that would bring these truths within the easy grasp of undeveloped minds, it is the old repeated tale? The Struggle between Right and Wrong. "Faust and Marguerite." The Wicked Punished, The Virtuous Rewarded.

Disguise them as you will, there are certain tendons which run through the world from age to age; cords which no human hand has yet severed—which no decree of God's has changed—these are love and death, hate and vengeance, virtue and vice, right and wrong, suffering and joy; and as long as there is a world, as long as children are born, parents will invent fables with which to bring these facts before their offsprings' eyes in an intelligible manner.

In the fables of the East, and especially of India, there is one peculiarity, namely, that craft and cunning are more generally rewarded than virtue, and stupidity condemned. This is the national characteristic. The tales of Southern India are as varied as any others, either Eastern or European. Magic and supernatural phenomena play a great part, but are usually assisted by the powers of the gods. This is again a national Hindoo characteristic. The Hindoo would shrink from any undertaking that is not under the patronage of the gods; yet here is a very noticeable feature, namely, that the divinities are treated as entirely secondary in power, interwoven only into a man's daily affairs as a sort of backbone or support in time of need, but to be despised and trampled upon at other times with impunity. This is a natural feature in a nation which has a deity to represent every vice and sin, and lends a certain character to the tales of Southern India different to the folklore of other countries.

Probably further research will lay bare many still hidden treasures of Hindoo folklore; but this small collection of tales will doubtless suffice to throw light on Indian tradition, and to bring forward the natural peculiarities of the Hindoos as well as the assimilation of the folklore of different nations, an assimilation which I maintain results from the teaching propensities of each country and not from appropriation.

GEORGIANA KINGSCOTE.

# FOLKLORE IN SOUTHERN INDIA.

## CHAPTER I.

### THE STORY OF THE THREE DEAF MEN.

When any awkward blunder occurs from a person acting under a mistaken notion, there is a common proverb in Tamil to the effect that the matter ended like the story of the three deaf men—(*Muchchevidan kadaiyây mudindadu*). The following is the story told to explain the allusion:—

In a remote village there lived a husband and wife. Both of them were quite deaf. They had made this household arrangement, namely, to cook cabbage with tamarind and soup without tamarind one day, and cabbage without tamarind and soup with tamarind on the other. Thus on every alternate day the same dishes were repeated. One day, when taking his meal, the husband found the tamarind cabbage so very tasty that he wanted to have it also next day, and gave instructions to that effect. The deaf wife did not understand the order. According to the established rule she cooked cabbage without tamarind next day. The husband, when he sat down to his meal, found his order disregarded and, being enraged thereat, threw the cabbage against the wall, and went out in a rage. The wife ate her fill, and prepared tamarind cabbage for her husband.

The husband went out, and sat down in a place where three roads crossed, to calm down his anger. At that time a shepherd happened to pass that way. He had lately lost a good cow and calf of his, and had been seeking them for some days. When he saw the deaf man sitting by the way, he took him for a soothsayer, and asked him to find out by his knowledge of *Jôsyam*[1] where the cow was likely to be found. The herdsman, too, was very deaf; and the man, without hearing what he was saying, abused him, and wished to be left undisturbed. In abusing him the husband stretched out his hand, pointing to the shepherd's face. This pointing the shepherd understood to indicate the direction where the lost cow and calf would be found. Thus thinking the poor shepherd went on in that direction, promising to present the soothsayer with the calf if he found it there with the cow. To his joy, and by mere chance, he found them. His delight knew no bounds. "That is a capital soothsayer. Surely I must present him with the calf." So thought he to himself, and returned with them to the deaf man, and, pointing to the calf, requested him to accept it.

---

[1] Soothsaying.

Now it unfortunately happened that the calf's tail was broken and crooked. The man thought the herdsman was blaming him unreasonably for having broken the calf's tail, while he knew nothing about it, and so, by a waive of his hand, denied the charge. This the shepherd mistook for a refusal of the calf, and a demand for the cow. The shepherd said, "How very greedy you are! I promised you only the calf, and not the cow." The husband said, "Never; I know nothing of either your cow or calf. I never broke the calf's tail. Some other must have done it." Thus they quarrelled, without understanding each other, for a long time, when a third party happened to pass by. Understanding the cause of the dispute, and, desiring to profit by their stupidity, he interfered, and said in a loud voice, and yet so as not to be heard by the deaf husband, "Well, shepherd, you had better go away with the cow. These soothsayers are always greedy. Leave the calf with me, and I shall make him accept it." The shepherd, much pleased to have secured the cow, walked home, leaving the calf with the third person. When the shepherd had gone, the passenger said to the deaf man, "You see how very unlawful it is for the shepherd to charge you with an offence which you never committed. It is always the case with shepherds. They are the biggest fools in the world! But never mind, so long as you have a friend in me. I shall somehow explain to him your innocence, and restore the calf to him." The husband, much pleased, ran home to escape from the consequences of supposed guilt. At the expense of the stupidity and deafness of both, the third traveller walked home with the calf.

The husband, on his return, sat down to his dinner, and his wife served him the tamarind cabbage. He happened to put his finger to the place where the cabbage without tamarind had previously been served on the leaf. On applying it to his mouth, he found it so very sweet that he demanded that dish again. The wife replied to him that she had already emptied the pan. "Then at least bring me the cabbage that is sticking to the saucepan," said the husband; and the wife did accordingly.

Here ends the story. The latter portion is also said to be the explanation of a proverb that is prevalent in Tamil,—"*Śevuru kîraiyai vaḷichchu pôḍuḍi śuṇaikeṭṭa mûḷi*," meaning, "O thou feelingless deaf woman, give me at least the cabbage that is sticking to the saucepan." This proverb is applied to stubborn wives, who will have their own way, and do not obey their husbands submissively in unrefined society.

## CHAPTER II.

## WHY BRÂHMAṆS CANNOT EAT IN THE DARK.

Among Hindûs, especially among Brâhmaṇs of the Madras Presidency—and I now see from personal observation that it is the same in the Bombay Presidency also—there is a custom, while taking their meals, of leaving their food uneaten when it so happens that from any cause the light is blown out. Of course this could occur only in the night-time. Such mishaps now-a-days take place only in poor families, sitting down to supper with a single light. Hence the following story, told as the origin of this custom, is beginning to be forgotten. It runs as follows:—

In a certain village there lived a Brâhmaṇ who had an only daughter. She was deeply read in Saṅskṛit, and was of the most charming beauty. He procured a husband for her as deeply read as herself. The betrothal had already taken place; the *muhûrta* or auspicious time for her marriage was fixed at the tenth *ghaṭikâ*[2] of that night. On that very evening the son-in-law went to a tank to perform his *Sandhyâ vandana* or evening prayers. It swarmed with crocodiles. People never went near it. The son-in-law, being quite new to the village, entered the tank without knowing anything of the danger. Unfortunately, there was none near to warn him. He had set his foot in the water when a crocodile caught him by the leg, and began to drag him into the water. That very night was fixed for his nuptials, and a crocodile was taking him to feast on his flesh. He was extremely horrified at his position, and said humbly to his enemy, "My friend crocodile! Listen to my words first, and then decide for yourself. A wife, the only daughter of an old Brâhmaṇ, is waiting for me to-night. If you eat me now, you take me away without my seeing her, my father-in-law, and other relatives. Their hearts may break at the news of my death on the very day of the wedding. They may all curse you. If, on the contrary, you leave me now, I shall go home, speak to my wife and others about the sad calamity that has come over me, and after embracing and taking leave of her will come to you for your supper at the fifteenth *ghaṭikâ*. Till then leave me." The cruel crocodile, though very fond of human flesh, and himself dying of hunger, spared him for a few *ghaṭikâs* at his humble request. After extracting several oaths from him that he would return in accordance to his promise, the crocodile went into the water.

The son-in-law also went home. All his joy vanished; how could he be happy after his promise to the crocodile. Still, to give no uneasiness to the aged parents of his wife, he underwent all the ceremonies of the marriage. Only five more *ghaṭikâs* remained for him to live in the world, as he thought. He, in a few words, explained

[2] An Indian hour equal to twenty-four minutes.

everything to his wife, and asked her permission to leave her. She showed no sign of sorrow, preached to him about the iron hand of fate, and that he must undergo what was written on his forehead. She most willingly gave him permission to go, and he returned to the tank even a *ghaṭikâ* earlier, and called the crocodile, who came and seized him.

At this moment a certain light glittered before the eyes of the crocodile and vanished. It was a woman that did it. The wife, after consoling her husband, and preaching to him about the supremacy of fate, had accompanied him unobserved with a lighted lamp concealed in a vessel. Just when the crocodile applied its teeth to the leg of her husband, she took the lamp out, flashed it before the crocodile's eyes, and quenched it. Nor was it without its intended effect. The crocodile left the husband to himself, and said, "You had better go now; I will never touch you after seeing a lamp extinguished when I began my meal to-day." The husband was astonished at the device of his wife, and still more at the faithful observance of a rule in an unreasonable beast. From that day it was fixed that men, who are still more reasonable, should never eat when the lamp is blown out.

Another story is told. In a remote village there lived a poor woman, who laboured from morning till night in different houses, and returned to her hut with two measures of rice. That quantity would serve for ten ordinary persons. Being extremely poor, she used to keep no lamp, but cook her rice in the dark, only guided by the light of the fire. When she sat down for her meal even the light of the fire faded; so she had to eat in the dark. Though she used the full two measures of rice that she brought away every day, her hunger was never satisfied; she was always in extreme want.

Now it so happened that she had a younger sister, who was somewhat richer than herself. The younger came to see her elder sister. The former never used to be without a light, and so asked her sister to buy some oil that night and light a lamp. The elder was compelled by necessity to do so; for that, she devoted a portion of her two measures of rice, and returned home with great uneasiness and perplexity of mind as to how less than two measures would furnish their supper that night, while full two measures were found insufficient on former occasions for herself alone. The lamp was set for the first time in her house, and she cooked the remaining rice. The younger sister was astonished to see her using so much for two. The elder, thinking within herself that the younger would soon see her mistake, cooked everything. Two leaves were spread, and they sat down to their supper.[3] Not even a fourth part of the rice in the pot was consumed, but already they were satisfied. The younger sister laughed at the foolishness of her elder, who now said, "I do not know what magic you have in you. Every day I cook two measures of rice, and fast the whole night, without finding them sufficient for myself. Now a fourth of less than two measures has satiated both. Please explain the cause." The younger sister, who was very intelligent herself, wanted to find out the cause, and asked next day if she might serve the meals without the lamp. Instead of eating she stretched out her hand and caught hold of a lock of hair. She asked the other at once to light the lamp, which, being done, they found a devil sitting by their side.

[3] It is the custom amongst widows to use betel leaves instead of plates.

On being questioned how he came there, he said that he was in the habit of going to every one who ate without a lamp, and swallowing his meals fast without leaving him a morsel. The elder sister perceived her mistake, and used a lamp from that day. The demon ceased to come. She had abundance for herself and something to spare. So when the lamp is blown out, devils are said to come and eat out of our leaves. Hence the custom of rising whenever such mishaps occur.

# CHAPTER III.

## THE SOOTHSAYER'S SON.

जन्मप्रभृति दारिद्र्यं दशवर्षाणि बन्धनम् ।
समुद्रतीरे मरणं किञ्चित् भोगं भविष्यति ॥

Thus a Soothsayer when on his death-bed wrote the horoscope of his second son, and bequeathed it to him as his only property, leaving the whole of his estate to his eldest son. The second son pondered over the horoscope, and fell into the following reflections:—

"Alas, am I born to this only in the world? The sayings of my father never failed. I have seen them prove true to the last word while he was living; and how has he fixed my horoscope! *Janma parabhṛiti dâridryam!* From my birth poverty! Nor is that my only fate. *Daśa varshâṇi bandhanam*: for ten years, imprisonment—a fate harder than poverty; and what comes next? *Samudratîrê maraṇam*: death on the sea-shore; which means that I must die away from home, far from friends and relatives on a sea-coast. The misery has reached its extreme height here. Now comes the funniest part of the horoscope, *Kiñchit bhôgam bhavishyati*—that I am to have some happiness afterwards! What this happiness is, is an enigma to me: To die first, to be happy for some time after! What happiness? Is it the happiness of this world? So it must be. For however clever one may be, he cannot foretell what may take place in the other world. Therefore it must be the happiness of this world; and how can that be possible after my death? It is impossible. I think my father has only meant this as a consoling conclusion to the series of calamities that he has prophesied. Three portions of his prophecy must prove true; the fourth and last is a mere comforting statement to bear patiently the calamities enumerated, and never to prove true. Therefore let me go to Bânâras, bathe in the holy Gaṅgâ, wash away my sins, and prepare myself for my end. Let me avoid sea-coasts, lest death meet me there in accordance with my father's words. Come imprisonment: I am prepared for it for ten years."

Thus thought he, and after all the funeral obsequies of his father were over, took leave of his elder brother, and started for Bânâras.[4] He went by the middle of the Dakhaṇ,[5] avoiding both the coasts, and went on journeying and journeying for weeks and months, till at last he reached the Vindhya mountains. While passing that desert he had to journey for a couple of days through a sandy plain, with no signs of life or vegetation. The little store of provision with which he was

[4] In English, Benares.

[5] The Deccan.

provided for a couple of days, at last was exhausted. The *chombu*,[6] which he carried always full, replenishing it with the sweet water from the flowing rivulet or plenteous tank, he had exhausted in the heat of the desert. There was not a morsel in his hand to eat; nor a drop of water to drink. Turn his eyes wherever he might he found a vast desert, out of which he saw no means of escape. Still he thought within himself, "Surely my father's prophecy never proved untrue. I must survive this calamity to find my death on some sea-coast." So thought he, and this thought gave him strength of mind to walk fast and try to find a drop of water somewhere to slake his dry throat. At last he succeeded, or rather thought that he succeeded. Heaven threw in his way a ruined well. He thought that he could collect some water if he let down his *chombu* with the string that he always carried noosed to the neck of it. Accordingly he let it down; it went some way and stopped, and the following words came from the well, "Oh, relieve me! I am the king of tigers, dying here of hunger. For the last three days I have had nothing. Fortune has sent you here. If you assist me now you will find a sure help in me throughout your life. Do not think that I am a beast of prey. When you have become my deliverer I can never touch you. Pray, kindly lift me up." Gaṅgâdhara, for that was the name of the Soothsayer's second son, found himself in a very perplexing position. "Shall I take him out or not? If I take him out he may make me the first morsel of his hungry mouth. No; that he will not do. For my father's prophecy never came untrue. I must die on a sea-coast and not by a tiger." Thus thinking, he asked the tiger king to hold tight to the vessel, which he accordingly did, and he lifted him up slowly. The tiger reached the top of the well and felt himself on safe ground. True to his word he did no harm to Gaṅgâdhara. On the other hand, he walked round his patron three times, and standing before him, humbly spoke the following words:—"My life-giver, my benefactor! I shall never forget this day, when I regained my life through your kind hands. In return for this kind assistance I pledge my oath to stand by you in all calamities. Whenever you are in any difficulty just think of me. I am there with you ready to oblige you by all the means that I can. To tell you briefly how I came in here:—Three days ago I was roaming in yonder forest, when I saw a goldsmith passing through it. I chased him. He, finding it impossible to escape my claws, jumped into this well, and is living to this moment in the very bottom of it. I also jumped in, but found myself in the first storey;[7] he is on the last and fourth storey. In the second storey lives a serpent half-famished with hunger. In the third storey lies a rat, similarly half-famished, and when you again begin to draw water these may request you first to release them. In the same way the goldsmith also may request. I tell you, as your bosom friend, never assist that wretched man, though he is your relation as a human being. Goldsmiths are never to be trusted. You can place more faith in me, a tiger, though I feast sometimes upon men, in a serpent whose sting makes your blood cold the very next moment, or in a rat, which does a thousand pieces of mischief in your house. But never trust a goldsmith. Do not release him; and if you do, you shall surely repent

[6] A small vessel.

[7] Storey is here put for divisions in an Indian well. These divisions are little projecting ledges of stone made for natives to stand on so that they can get down close to the water if the well is not full. There are sometimes six or seven divisions, or ledges, of this sort.

of it one day or other." Thus advising, the hungry tiger went away without waiting for an answer.

Gaṅgâdhara thought several times of the eloquent way in which the tiger addressed him, and admired his fluency of speech. His thirst was not quenched. So he let down his vessel again, which was now caught hold of by the serpent, who addressed him thus:—"Oh my protector! Lift me up. I am the king of serpents, and the son of Âdiśêsha,[8] who is now pining away in agony for my disappearance. Release me now. I shall ever remain your servant, remember your assistance, and help you throughout life in all possible ways. Oblige me: I am dying." Gaṅgâdhara, calling again to mind the *Samudratîrê maraṇam*—death on the sea-shore—lifted him up. He, like the tiger-king, walked round him thrice, and prostrating himself before him spoke thus:—"Oh, my life-giver, my father, for so I must call you, as you have given me another birth. I have already told you that I am Âdiśêsha's son, and that I am the king of serpents. I was three days ago basking myself in the morning sun, when I saw a rat running before me. I chased him. He fell into this well. I followed him, but instead of falling on the third storey where he is now lying, I fell into the second. It was on the same evening that the goldsmith also fell down into the fourth storey, and the tiger whom you released just before me fell down into the first. What I have to tell you now is—do not relieve the goldsmith, though you may release the rat. As a rule, goldsmiths are never to be trusted. I am going away now to see my father. Whenever you are in any difficulty just think of me. I will be there by your side to assist you by all possible means. If, notwithstanding my repeated advice, you happen to release the goldsmith, you shall suffer for it severely." So saying, the Nâgarâja (serpent-king) glided away in zigzag movements, and was out of sight in a moment.

The poor son of the Soothsayer who was now almost dying of thirst, and was even led to think that the messengers of death were near him, notwithstanding his firm belief in the words of his father let down his vessel for a third time. The rat caught hold of it, and without discussing, he lifted up the poor animal at once. But it would not go away without showing its gratitude—"Oh life of my life! My benefactor! I am the king of rats. Whenever you are in any calamity just think of me. I will come to you, and assist you. My keen ears overheard all that the tiger-king and serpent-king told you about the Svarṇataskara[9] (*gold-smith*), who is in the fourth storey. It is nothing but a sad truth that goldsmiths ought never to be trusted. Therefore never assist him as you have done to us all. And if you do, you shall feel it. I am hungry; let me go for the present." Thus taking leave of his benefactor, the rat, too, ran away.

Gaṅgâdhara for a while thought upon the repeated advice given by the three animals about releasing the goldsmith, "What wrong would there be in my assisting him? Why should I not release him also?" So thinking to himself, Gaṅgâdhara let down the vessel again. The goldsmith caught hold of it, and demanded help.

[8] The first serpent—the king of serpents.

[9] Literally the stealer of gold—a practice very common in India among that class. There is a proverb to the effect that even from the gold given by their mothers to be turned into jewels, they will pilfer a little.

The Soothsayer's son had no time to lose; he was himself dying of thirst. Therefore he lifted the goldsmith up, who now began his story:—"Stop for a while," said Gaṅgâdhara, and after quenching his thirst by letting down his vessel for the fifth time, still fearing that some one might remain in the well and demand his assistance, he listened to the goldsmith, who began as follows:—"My dear friend, my protector, what a deal of nonsense these brutes have been talking to you about me; I am glad you have not followed their advice. I am just now dying of hunger. Permit me to go away. My name is Mâṇikkâśâri. I live in the East main street of Ujjaini which is twenty *kâs*[10] to the south of this place, and so lies on your way when you return from Bânâras. Do not forget to come to me and receive my kind remembrances of your assistance, on your way back to your country." So saying the goldsmith took his leave, and Gaṅgâdhara also pursued his way north after the above adventures.

He reached Bânâras, and lived there for more than ten years, spending his time in bathing, prayers, and other religious ceremonies. He quite forgot the tiger, serpent, rat, and goldsmith. After ten years of religious life, thoughts of home and of his brother rushed into his mind. "I have secured enough merit now by my religious observances. Let me return home." Thus thought Gaṅgâdhara within himself, and immediately he was on his way back to his country. Remembering the prophecy of his father he returned by the same way by which he went to Bânâras ten years before. While thus retracing his steps he reached the ruined well where he had released the three brute kings and the goldsmith. At once the old recollections rushed into his mind, and he thought of the tiger to test his fidelity. Only a moment passed, and the tiger-king came running before him carrying a large crown in his mouth, the glitter of the diamonds of which for a time outshone even the bright rays of the sun. He dropped the crown at his life-giver's feet, and putting aside all his pride, humbled himself like a pet cat to the strokes of his protector, and began in the following words:—"My life-giver! How is it that you have forgotten me, your poor servant, for such a long time? I am glad to find that I still occupy a corner in your mind. I can never forget the day when I owed my life to your lotus hands. I have several jewels with me of little value. This crown, being the best of all, I have brought here as a single ornament of great value, and hence easily portable and useful to you in your own country." Gaṅgâdhara looked at the crown, examined it over and over, counted and recounted the gems, and thought within himself that he would become the richest of men by separating the diamonds and gold, and selling them in his own country. He took leave of the tiger-king, and after his disappearance thought of the kings of serpents and rats, who came in their turns with their presents, and after the usual formalities and exchange of words took their leave. Gaṅgâdhara was extremely delighted at the faithfulness with which the brute beasts behaved themselves, and went on his way to the south. While going along he spoke to himself thus:—"These beasts have been so very faithful in their assistance. Much more, therefore, must Mâṇikkâśâri be faithful. I do not want anything from him now. If I take this crown with me as it is, it occupies much space in my bundle. It may also excite the curiosity of some robbers on the way. I will go now to Ujjaini on my way, Mâṇikkâśâri requested

[10] The distance of a *kâs* being equal to 2000 Indian poles.

me to see him without failure on my return journey. I shall do so, and request him to have the crown melted, the diamonds and gold separated. He must do that kindness at least for me. I shall then roll up these diamonds and gold ball in my rags, and bend my way homewards." Thus thinking and thinking he reached Ujjaini. At once he enquired for the house of his goldsmith friend, and found him without difficulty. Mâṇikkâśâri was extremely delighted to find on his threshold him who ten years before, notwithstanding the advice repeatedly given him by the sage-looking tiger, serpent, and rat, had relieved him from the pit of death. Gaṅgâdhara at once showed him the crown that he received from the tiger-king, told him how he got it, and requested his kind assistance to separate the gold and diamonds. Mâṇikkâśâri agreed to do so, and meanwhile asked his friend to rest himself for a while to have his bath and meals; and Gaṅgâdhara, who was very observant of his religious ceremonies, went direct to the river to bathe.

How came a crown in the jaws of a tiger? It is not a difficult question to solve. A king must have furnished the table of the tiger for a day or two. Had it not been for that, the tiger could not have had a crown with him. Even so it was. The king of Ujjaini had a week before gone with all his hunters on a hunting expedition. All of a sudden a tiger—as we know now, the very tiger-king himself—started from the wood, seized the king, and vanished. The hunters returned and informed the prince about the sad calamity that had befallen his father. They all saw the tiger carrying away the king. Yet such was their courage that they could not lift their weapons to bring to the prince the corpse at least of his father.

When they informed the prince about the death of his father he wept and wailed, and gave notice that he would give half of his kingdom to any one who should bring him news about the murderer of his father. The prince did not at all believe that his father was devoured by the tiger. His belief was that some hunters, coveting the ornaments on the king's person, had murdered him. Hence he had issued the notice. The goldsmith knew full well that it was a tiger that killed the king, and not any hunter's hands, since he had heard from Gaṅgâdhara about how he obtained the crown. Still, ambition to get half the kingdom prevailed, and he resolved with himself to make over Gaṅgâdhara as the king's murderer. The crown was lying on the floor where Gaṅgâdhara left it with his full confidence in Mâṇikkâśâri. Before his protector's return the goldsmith, hiding the crown under his garments, flew to the palace. He went before the prince and informed him that the assassin was caught, and placed the crown before him. The prince took it into his hands, examined it, and at once gave half the kingdom to Mâṇikkâśâri, and then enquired about the murderer. "He is bathing in the river, and is of such and such appearance," was the reply. At once four armed soldiers fly to the river, and bound the poor Brâhmaṇ hand and foot, he sitting in meditation the while, without any knowledge of the fate that hung over him. They brought Gaṅgâdhara to the presence of the prince, who turned his face away from the murderer or supposed murderer, and asked his soldiers to throw him into the *kârâgṛiham*.[11] In a minute, without knowing the cause, the poor Brâhmaṇ found himself in the dark caves of the *kârâgṛiham*.

[11] Dungeon.

In old times the *kârâgṛiham* answered the purposes of the modern jail. It was a dark cellar underground, built with strong stone walls, into which any criminal guilty of a capital offence was ushered to breathe his last there without food and drink. Such was the cellar into which Gaṅgâdhara was thrust. In a few hours after he left the goldsmith he found himself inside a dark cell stinking with human bodies, dying and dead. What were his thoughts when he reached that place? "It is the goldsmith that has brought me to this wretched state; and, as for the prince: Why should he not enquire as to how I obtained the crown? It is of no use to accuse either the goldsmith or the prince now. We are all the children of fate. We must obey her commands. *Daśavarshâṇi Bandhanam.* This is but the first day of my father's prophecy. So far his statement is true. But how am I going to pass ten years here? Perhaps without anything to sustain life I may drag on my existence for a day or two. But how pass ten years? That cannot be, and I must die. Before death comes let me think of my faithful brute friends."

So pondered Gaṅgâdhara in the dark cell underground, and at that moment thought of his three friends. The tiger-king, serpent-king, and rat-king assembled at once with their armies at a garden near the *kârâgṛiham,* and for a while did not know what to do. A common cause—how to reach their protector, who was now in the dark cell underneath—united them all. They held their council, and decided to make an underground passage from the inside of a ruined well to the *kârâgṛiham.* The rat *râjâ* issued an order at once to that effect to his army. They, with their nimble teeth, bored the ground a long way to the walls of the prison. After reaching it they found that their teeth could not work on the hard stones. The bandicoots were then specially ordered for the business; they, with their hard teeth, made a small slit in the wall for a rat to pass and repass without difficulty. Thus a passage was effected.

The rat *râjâ* entered first to condole with his protector on his misfortune. The king of the tigers sent word through the snake-king that he sympathised most sincerely with his sorrow, and that he was ready to render all help for his deliverance. He suggested a means for his escape also. The serpent *râjâ* went in, and gave Gaṅgâdhara hopes of delivery. The rat-king undertook to supply his protector with provisions. "Whatever sweetmeats or bread are prepared in any house, one and all of you must try to bring whatever you can to our benefactor. Whatever clothes you find hanging in a house, cut down, dip the pieces in water, and bring the wet bits to our benefactor. He will squeeze them and gather water for drink! and the bread and sweetmeats shall form his food." Having issued these orders the king of the rats, took leave of Gaṅgâdhara. They, in obedience to their king's order, continued to supply provisions and water.

The Nâgarâja said:—"I sincerely condole with you in your calamity; the tiger-king also fully sympathises with you, and wants me to tell you so, as he cannot drag his huge body here as we have done with our small ones. The king of the rats has promised to do his best to provide you with food. We would now do what we can for your release. From this day we shall issue orders to our armies to oppress all the subjects of this kingdom. The percentage of death by snake-bite and tigers shall increase from this day. And day by day it shall continue to increase till your release. After eating what the rats bring you, you had better take your seat near the entrance of the *kârâgṛiham*. Owing to the many sudden deaths that will occur some people that walk over the prison may say, 'How wicked the king has become. Were it not for his wickedness so many dreadful deaths by snake-bites could never occur.' Whenever you hear people speaking so, you had better bawl out so as to be heard by them, 'The wretched prince imprisoned me on the false charge of having killed his father, while it was a tiger that killed him. From that day these calamities have broken out in his dominions. If I were released I would save all by my powers of healing poisonous wounds and by incantations.' Some one may report this to the king, and if he knows it, you will obtain your liberty." Thus comforting his protector in trouble, he advised him to pluck up courage, and took leave of him. From that day tigers and serpents, acting under the special orders of their kings, united in killing as many persons and cattle as possible. Every day people were carried away by tigers or bitten by serpents. This havoc continued. Gaṅgâdhara went on roaring as loud he could that he would save those lives, had he only his liberty. Few heard him. The few that did took his words for the voice of a ghost. "How could he manage to live without food and drink for so long a time?" said the persons walking over his head to each other. Thus passed months and years. Gaṅgâdhara sat in the dark cellar, without the sun's light falling upon him, and feasted upon the bread-crumbs and sweetmeats that the rats so kindly supplied him with. These circumstances had completely changed his body. He had become a red, stout, huge, unwieldy lump of flesh. Thus passed full ten years, as prophesied in the horoscope—*Daśavarshâṇi Bandhanam.*

Ten complete years rolled away in close imprisonment. On the last evening of the tenth year one of the serpents got into the bed-chamber of the princess and sucked her life. She breathed her last. She was the only daughter of the king. He had no other issue—son or daughter. His only hope was in her; and she was snatched away by a cruel and untimely death. The king at once sent for all the snake-bite curers. He promised half his kingdom and his daughter's hand to him who would restore her to life. Now it was that a servant of the king, who had several times overheard Gaṅgâdhara's cries, reported the matter to him. The king at once ordered the cell to be examined. There was the man sitting in it. How has he managed to live so long in the cell? Some whispered that he must be a divine being. Some concluded that he must surely win the hand of the princess by restoring her to life. Thus they discussed, and the discussions brought Gaṅgâdhara to the king.

The king no sooner saw Gaṅgâdhara than he fell on the ground. He was struck by the majesty and grandeur of his person. His ten years' imprisonment in the deep cell underground had given a sort of lustre to his body, which was not to be met with in ordinary persons. His hair had first to be cut before his face could be seen. The king begged forgiveness for his former fault, and requested him to revive his daughter.

"Bring me in a *muhûrta*[12] all the corpses of men and cattle, dying and dead, that remain unburnt or unburied within the range of your dominions; I shall re-

[12] A period of time equal to an hour and a half.

vive them all," were the only words that Gaṅgâdhara spoke. After it he closed his lips as if in deep meditation, which commanded more respect than ever.

Cart-loads of corpses of men and cattle began to come in every minute. Even graves, it is said, were broken open, and corpses buried a day or two before were taken out and sent for the revival. As soon as all were ready, Gaṅgâdhara took a vessel full of water and sprinkled it over them all, thinking only of his Nâgarâja and Vyâghrarâja.[13] All rose up as if from deep slumber, and went to their respective homes. The princess, too, was restored to life. The joy of the king knew no bounds. He cursed the day on which he imprisoned him, blamed himself for having believed the word of a goldsmith, and offered him the hand of his daughter and the whole kingdom, instead of half as he promised. Gaṅgâdhara would not accept anything. The king requested him to put a stop for ever to these calamities. He agreed to do so, and asked the king to assemble all his subjects in a wood near the town. "I shall there call in all the tigers and serpents and give them a general order." So said Gaṅgâdhara, and the king accordingly gave the order. In a couple of *ghaṭikâs*[14] the wood near Ujjaini was full of people, who assembled to witness the authority of man over such enemies of human beings as tigers and serpents. "He is no man; be sure of that. How could he have managed to live for ten years without food and drink? He is surely a god." Thus speculated the mob.

When the whole town was assembled, just at the dusk of evening, Gaṅgâdhara sat dumb for a moment, and thought upon the Vyâghrarâja and Nâgarâja, who came running with all their armies. People began to take to their heels at the sight of tigers. Gaṅgâdhara assured them of safety, and stopped them.

The grey light of the evening, the pumpkin colour of Gaṅgâdhara, the holy ashes scattered lavishly over his body, the tigers and snakes humbling themselves at his feet, gave him the true majesty of the god Gaṅgâdhara.[15] For who else by a single word could thus command vast armies of tigers and serpents, said some among the people. "Care not for it; it may be by magic. That is not a great thing. That he revived cart-loads of corpses makes him surely Gaṅgâdhara," said others. The scene produced a very great effect upon the minds of the mob.

"Why should you, my children, thus trouble these poor subjects of Ujjaini? Reply to me, and henceforth desist from your ravages." Thus said the Soothsayer's son, and the following reply came from the king of the tigers; "Why should this base king imprison your honour, believing the mere word of a goldsmith that your honour killed his father? All the hunters told him that his father was carried away by a tiger. I was the messenger of death sent to deal the blow on his neck. I did it, and gave the crown to your honour. The prince makes no enquiry, and at once imprisons your honour. How can we expect justice from such a stupid king as that? Unless he adopts a better standard of justice we will go on with our destruction."

The king heard, cursed the day on which he believed in the word of a goldsmith, beat his head, tore his hair, wept and wailed for his crime, asked a thousand pardons, and swore to rule in a just way from that day. The serpent-king and ti-

[13] King of tigers.
[14] A *ghaṭikâ* is equal to twenty-four minutes.
[15] Śiva.

ger-king also promised to observe their oath as long as justice prevailed, and took their leave. The goldsmith fled for his life. He was caught by the soldiers of the king, and was pardoned by the generous Gaṅgâdhara, whose voice now reigned supreme. All returned to their homes.

The king again pressed Gaṅgâdhara to accept the hand of his daughter. He agreed to do so, not then, but some time afterwards. He wished to go and see his elder brother first, and then to return and marry the princess. The king agreed; and Gaṅgâdhara left the city that very day on his way home.

It so happened that unwittingly he took a wrong road, and had to pass near a sea coast. His elder brother was also on his way up to Bânâras by that very same route. They met and recognised each other, even at a distance. They flew into each other's arms. Both remained still for a time almost unconscious with joy. The emotion of pleasure (*ânanda*) was so great, especially in Gaṅgâdhara, that it proved dangerous to his life. In a word, he died of joy.

The sorrow of the elder brother could better be imagined than described. He saw again his lost brother, after having given up, as it were, all hopes of meeting him. He had not even asked him his adventures. That he should be snatched away by the cruel hand of death seemed unbearable to him. He wept and wailed, took the corpse on his lap, sat under a tree, and wetted it with tears. But there was no hope of his dead brother coming to life again.

The elder brother was a devout worshipper of Gaṇapati.[16] That was a Friday, a day very sacred to that god. The elder brother took the corpse to the nearest Gaṇêśa[17] temple and called upon him. The god came, and asked him what he wanted. "My poor brother is dead and gone; and this is his corpse. Kindly keep it in your charge till I finish worshipping you. If I leave it anywhere else the devils may snatch it away when I am absent worshipping you; after finishing your *pûjâ*[18] I shall burn him." Thus said the elder brother, and, giving the corpse to the god Gaṇêśa, he went to prepare himself for that deity's ceremonials. Gaṇêśa made over the corpse to his *Gaṇas*,[19] asking them to watch over it carefully.

So a spoiled child receives a fruit from its father, who, when he gives it the fruit asks the child to keep it safe. The child thinks within itself, "My father will forgive me if I eat a portion of it." So saying it eats a portion, and when it finds it so sweet, it eats the whole, saying, "Come what will, what can father do, after all, if I eat it? Perhaps give me a stroke or two on the back. Perhaps he may forgive me." In the same way these *Gaṇas* of Gaṇapati first ate a portion of the corpse, and when they found it sweet, for we know it was crammed up with the sweetmeats of the kind rats, devoured the whole, and began consulting about the best excuse possible to offer to their master.

The elder brother, after finishing the *pûjâ,* demanded his brother's corpse of the god. The god called his *Gaṇas* who came to the front blinking, and fearing the

[16] The eldest son of Śiva commonly known as the belly god.

[17] Another name of Gaṇapati.

[18] Worship.

[19] Attendants of Gaṇêśa.

anger of their master. The god was greatly enraged. The elder brother was very angry. When the corpse was not forthcoming he cuttingly remarked, "Is this, after all, the return for my deep belief in you? You are unable even to return my brother's corpse." Gaṇêśa was much ashamed at the remark, and at the uneasiness that he had caused to his worshipper. So he, by his divine power, gave him a living Gaṅgâdhara instead of the dead corpse. Thus was the second son of the Soothsayer restored to life.

The brothers had a long talk about each other's adventures. They both went to Ujjaini, where Gaṅgâdhara married the princess, and succeeded to the throne of that kingdom. He reigned for a long time, conferring several benefits upon his brother. How is the horoscope to be interpreted? A special synod of Soothsayers was held. A thousand emendations were suggested. Gaṅgâdhara would not accept them. At last one Soothsayer cut the knot by stopping at a different place in reading, "*Samudra tîrê maraṇam kiñchit*." "On the sea-shore death for *some time*. Then "*Bhôgam bhavishyati*." "There shall be happiness for the person concerned." Thus the passage was interpreted. "Yes; my father's words never went wrong," said Gaṅgâdhara. The three brute kings continued their visits often to the Soothsayer's son, the then king of Ujjaini. Even the faithless goldsmith became a frequent visitor at the palace, and a receiver of several benefits from royal hands.

# CHAPTER IV.

## RAṆAVÎRASIṄG.

Once upon a time in the town of Vañjaimânagar,[20] there ruled a king, named Śivâchâr. He was a most just king, and ruled so well that no stone thrown up fell down, no crow pecked at the new drawn milk, the lion and the bull drank water from the same pond, and peace and prosperity reigned throughout the kingdom. Notwithstanding all these blessings, care always sat on his face. The fruit which makes life in this world sweet, the redeemer to him from the horrible *Naraka* of *Put*,[21] a Putra,[22] he had not. His days and nights he spent in praying that God might bless him with a son. Wherever he saw *pîpal* trees (*Aśvattharâjas*),[23] he ordered Brâhmaṇs to surround them. Whatever medicines the doctors recommended he was ever ready to swallow, however bitter they might be. "Eat even dung to get a son," says the proverb, and accordingly he did every thing to secure that happiness, but all in vain.

Śivâchâr had a minister, named Kharavadana, a most wicked tyrant as ever lived in the world. The thought that the king was without an heir, and had no hopes of one, awakened in his mind the ambition of securing for his family the throne of Vañjaimânagar. Śivâchâr knew this well. But what could he do. His only care was to send up additional prayers to frustrate the thoughts of Kharavadana, and to secure for himself a good position after death, without undergoing the severe torments of the *Put*-hell.

At last fortune favoured Śivâchâr; for what religious man fails to secure his desire? The king in his sixtieth year had a son. His joy can better be imagined than described. Lacs (Lâkhs) of Brâhmaṇs were fed in honour of the son-birth festival, *Putrôtsavam*, as it is technically called. The state prisons were opened, and all the prisoners let loose. Thousands of kine and innumerable acres of land were offered to Brâhmaṇs, and every kind of charity was duly practised. The ten days of the *Sûtikâgṛihavâsa* (confinement) were over. On the eleventh day the father saw his much longed-for son's face, and read on the lines of it great prosperity, learning, valour, goodness and every excellent quality.

The cradle-swinging, naming, and other ceremonies were duly performed,

[20] Classical name of Karûr, a small, but very ancient, town in the Kôyambatûr District of the Madras Presidency.

[21] *Naraka of Put*—*Naraka* is hell, and *Put* is a certain kind of hell to which, according to Hindû mythology, son-less persons are hurled down.

[22] *Putra*-son, so-called as he protects the father from the hell of *Put*.

[23] *Ficus religiosa.*

and the prince grew up under the great care generally shown to a king's son. His name the elders fixed as Sundara.[24] The minister whose only wish was to get the throne for his family, was much disappointed at the birth of a son to his master. The whole kingdom rejoiced at the event, and the minister was the only man who was sorry. When one is disappointed in his high hopes and expectations, he devises plans to take away the barrier that lies in his way. Even so, Kharavadana said to himself, "Let me see how affairs progress. The old king is near his grave. When he dies, leaving a son in his minority I myself must be his regent for a time. Shall I not then have opportunity enough of securing for ever for myself and my family the throne of Vañjaimânagar?" So thought he within himself, and was quiet for a time.

Śivâchâr, who was a very shrewd man, on several occasions, read the minister's mind, and knew very well how his intentions stood. "This cruel devil may murder my only son. I care not if he usurps the throne. What I fear is, that he may murder him. *Na daivam Śaṅkarât param.* No other god but Śaṅkara. And he must have his own way. If it is so written on the prince's head I cannot avoid it." Thus sighed Śivâchâr, and this sorrow (*śôka*), made him leaner day by day. Just ten years after the birth of Sundara, the king fell ill and lay on his deathbed.

Śivâchâr had a servant, named Raṇavîrasiṅg, whom he had all along observed to be very honest and faithful. That servant the king called to his side, and asking all others except Sundara, who was weeping by his father's pillow, to leave the room, addressed him thus:—"My dear Raṇavîrasiṅg! I have only a few *ghaṭikâs* before me. Listen to my words, and act accordingly. There is one God above us all, who will punish or reward us according to our bad or good acts. If by avarice or greed of money you ever play false to the trust that I am going to repose in you that God will surely punish you. It is not unknown to you what great difficulties I had in getting this only son, Sundara; how many temples I built, how many Brâhmaṇs I fed, how many religious austerities I underwent, &c., &c.. God after all gave me a son." Here his sorrow prevented him from proceeding further, and he began to cry aloud, and shed tears. "Do not weep on my account, father. We cannot wipe off what was written on our heads. We must undergo happiness or misery as is thereon written by Brahmâ, cried the prince. Raṇavîrasiṅg was melted at the sight. He took the boy on his lap, and with his own upper garment wiped his eyes. The old man continued, "Thus you, my faithful Raṇavîrasiṅg, know everything. I now wish that I had not performed all that I did to get this son. For when I die at this moment, who is there to take care of him for the next? Kharavadana may devise plan after plan to remove my boy from this world, and secure the kingdom for himself. My only hope is in you. I give him into your hands." Here the aged father, notwithstanding his illness, rose up a little from his bed, took hold of his son's hand, and after kissing it for the last time, placed it in Raṇavîrasiṅg's. "Care not if he does not get the kingdom. If you only preserve him from the wicked hands of the minister whom I have all along seen to be covetous of the throne, you will do a great work for your old master. I make you from this moment the lord of my palace. From this minute you are father, mother, brother, servant, and everything to my son. Take care that you do not betray your trust." Thus ended the king, and

[24] The fair.

sent at once for the minister. When he came he spoke to him thus, "Kharavadana! See what I am now. Yesterday I was on the throne. To-day, in a few minutes, I must breathe my last. Such is the uncertainty of life. Man's good acts alone follow him to the other world. Take my signet-ring. [Here the king took the ring from off his finger, and gave it to the minister.] Yours is the throne for the present, as long as the prince is in his minority. Govern well the kingdom. When the prince attains his sixteenth year kindly give him back the throne. Exercise a paternal care over him. Find a good and intelligent princess for his wife." Suddenly, before his speech was quite finished, the king felt the last pangs of death. The sage-looking minister promised him everything.

Śivâchâr breathed his last. After the usual weeping and wailing of a Hindû funeral, his corpse was burnt to ashes in a sandalwood pyre. All his queens—and there were several scores—committed *satî*[25] with the corpse. The ceremonies were all regularly conducted, the minister himself superintended everything.

Kharavadana then succeeded to the throne of Vañjaimânagar. Raṇavîrasiṅg became the lord of the palace, and true to his promise exercised all care over his trust. He was always at the side of Sundara. That he might not lose the sweetness of boyhood in study and play, Raṇavîrasiṅg brought to the palace twenty gentlemen's sons of good conduct and learning and made them the prince's fellow-students. A professor for every branch of learning was employed to teach the prince and his companions. Sundara thus received a sound and liberal education, only he was never allowed to go out of the palace. Raṇavîrasiṅg guarded him very strictly, and he had every reason to do so. For Kharavadana, as soon as he became king, had issued a notice that the assassin of Sundara should have a reward of a *karôr*[26] mohurs; and already every avaricious hand was in search of his head. Before the issue of this notice, Kharavadana found out a good girl and married her to the prince. She lived with her husband in the palace, and Raṇavîrasiṅg strictly watched her, as she had been chosen by the minister. He would not allow Sundara to speak to her. These strict prohibitions displeased the prince, even with his faithful servant. But the latter could not help it till he had full confidence in her. He used to advise Sundara not even to take a betel-leaf from her hands. But love is blind. So the prince within himself accused his old guardian; but he could not help following his orders. Thus passed on a few years.

Sundara reached his sixteenth year. Nothing happened about the transference of the kingdom; the prince, almost in imprisonment in the palace, had forgotten everything about the kingdom. Raṇavîrasiṅg wished to wait till, as he thought, the prince had acquired better governing faculties. Thus some time passed.

Full eight years had elapsed from the death of Śivâchâr. Sundara was already eighteen, and still he had not received his kingdom. Nothing was neglected in his education. Though Raṇavîrasiṅg exercised all paternal care over him, still it was not to his liking; for he found in him a great barrier to the pleasures of youth. The only pleasure for the prince, therefore, was the company of his friends.

[25] Voluntary cremation of widows with the dead bodies of their husbands on the funeral pile.

[26] *Karôr* is equal to ten lacs (*lâkhs*); *mohur* is an old gold coin.

One fine evening on the fourteenth day of the dark half of the month of Vaiśâkha of the *Vasanta*[27] season, the prince was sitting with his companions in the seventh story of his mansion viewing the town. The dusk of evening was just throwing her mantle over the city. People in their several vocations were at that time ceasing work, and returning home. In the eastern division of the town the prince saw a big mansion, and just to break the silence asked his friends what that was. "That is the Râjasthânik Kachêri,[28] a place you ought to have been sitting in for the last two years. The wretched minister, Kharavadana, has already usurped your seat; for, if he had intended to give you back the kingdom he would have done it two years ago when you reached your sixteenth year. Let us now console ourselves that God has spared your life till now, notwithstanding all the awards promised to the taker of your head. Even the proclamation is dying out of the memory of the people now." So said one of his friends and ceased.

These words fell like arrows in the ear of Sundara and troubled him. Shame that he had been thus treated brought a change of colour over his face which all his friends perceived, and they felt sorry for having touched upon the subject. The prince, perceiving that he had played a woman's part among his friends, resumed or pretended to resume his former cheerful countenance, and changed the conversation to some pleasanter topics. They separated very late that night. Before doing so, Sundara asked them all to present themselves in the *durbâr* hall[29] early next morning. At the same time he also ordered Raṇavîrasiṅg to keep horses ready for himself and his friends for a morning ride through the town the next day. "I was only waiting to hear such an order from your own mouth, *Mai Bâb Chakravarti*![30] I was thinking from your retired disposition that you were not an energetic man. I will have the horses ready." Raṇavîrasiṅg at once issued orders to his servants to keep ready saddled and decked twenty-one horses for the prince and his companions. He also appointed a certain number of his men to ride in front of the party.

The morning came. The friends assembled, as promised the previous evening. The prince and they, after a light breakfast, mounted their horses. The horsemen rode in front and behind. The prince with his friends marched in the middle. Raṇavîrasiṅg with drawn sword rode by his side. The party went through the four main streets of the town. Every one rose up and paid due respect to their old king's son. When passing through the street where the minister's mansion was, Raṇavîrasiṅg perceived that Kharavadana paid no respect to the royal march. This seemed a most unbearable insult to Raṇavîrasiṅg. He bit his lips, gnashed his teeth, and wrung his hands. The prince observed all the mental pains of his faithful guardian, and laughed to himself at his simplicity. About mid-day the party returned to the palace. The friends dispersed, and Sundara after the ceremonies of the new-moon day had a slight dinner, and retired to rest.

The morning ride was deep in the mind of the prince. Though he laughed to himself at the simplicity of Raṇavîrasiṅg when the latter gnashed his teeth in

[27] Spring.
[28] The king's court.
[29] Council chamber.
[30] My darling prince.

the morning, the insult had left a stronger and deeper impression in his heart. The day was almost spent. Sundara took a very light supper, and shut himself up in his bed-room before the first watch was quite over. Raṇavîrasiṅg, as usual, watched outside. The prince found his wife sound asleep in her bed, and without disturbing her he went up and down the room. A thread-like substance attracted his attention in a corner of the bed-chamber. On examination he found it to be a thread ladder. He had not even time to think how it came into the bed-chamber. Just then Raṇavîrasiṅg had retired for a few minutes to take his supper. "The old fool is off now to eat; and Paramêśvara has thrown this ladder in my way. Let me now escape." Thus thinking, Sundara came out unobserved by his old guardian, and ascended to the top of the seventh mansion. From that place he cast his ladder towards a big tree in the East Main street. On pulling it he found that it was firmly fixed. "Let me get down, and Paramêśvara will assist me." So praying, before the first watch was over, the prince got down from his palace, and was in a few minutes in the East street. The severe watch kept over him by Raṇavîrasiṅg made it very difficult for him to go out when he liked, and now by the grace of God, as he thought, he had escaped that dark new-moon night.

"Life is dear to every one. What can I do if any of the minister's men find me out now and murder me? *Na daivam Śaṅkarât param.* No god but Śaṅkara, and he will now help me." Thus thinking he walked to the nearest pyal, and lingered there till the bustle of the town subsided. Nor was it in vain that he stopped there. He overheard while there the following conversation take place between the master and mistress of the house at which he lingered:—"Console yourself, my wife. What shall we do? Fate has so willed it on our heads. May Brahmâ[31] become without a temple for the evil that he has sent us. When the old king was living he appreciated my merits, and at every *Saṅkrânti*[32] gave me due *dakshiṇâ*[33] for my knowledge of the *Vêdas*.[34] Now there reigns a tyrant over our kingdom. I have been lingering here with the hope that the son of Śivâchâr would one day come to the throne and relieve our sufferings. Now that such hope is altogether gone, I have made up my mind to leave this nasty city, and go to some good place where there reigns a king who can appreciate our *yôgyatâ* (merit)." Of these words Sundara overheard every syllable, and these supplied the fuel to the fire of shame and anger that was already burning in his mind. "Let me try to win back my kingdom. If I succeed, I shall save other lives. If I die, I alone die. May Paramêśvara help me." So saying he walked out of the town, and passed the east gate. The night was as dark as could be, for it was a new moon night. Clouds were gathering in the sky, and there were some symptoms of rain.

There was a Gaṇêśa temple on the way. As it was already drizzling, the prince went inside till the rain should cease. No sooner had he entered it than he saw two men, who by their conversation appeared to be shepherds, coming towards that same temple. They seemed to have been watching their flocks near an adjacent field, and had come to shelter themselves from the rain in the temple. Sundara

[31] The creator of the Hindu mythology.

[32] A Hindû feast.

[33] Fee.

[34] *Vêdas*—The sacred books of the Hindûs.

when he saw them, trembled for his life, and crept in. The shepherds sat down on the verandah, and taking out their bags began to chew betel-nuts. An idle lizard began to chirp in a corner. To break the silence, one said to the other, "Well, Râmakôn, I have heard that you are a great soothsayer and interpreter of bird sounds and lizard speeches. Let me know what these chirps of the lizard that we heard just now mean. Tell me." Râmakôn replied, "This is news which I would never have revealed at any other time. But as no fourth person is likely to be here at this time on a rainy night, let me tell you that the prince of the town is now lingering here in this temple. So the lizard says. Hence I said, 'no fourth person.' I am glad that no evil hand has yet been tempted, though such a high price has been set upon his head. The very fact that he has lived up to this time unhurt in a tiger's domain augurs well for his future prosperity." Râmakôn had scarcely finished his speech when the idle lizard again made its chit, chit, and Râmakôn now asked his friend, Lakshmaṇakôn, for that was the other's name, to interpret those sounds. "This has rather a sad meaning for the prince. The Mantrî[35] and Pradhânî[36] are coming here in a few minutes (*nimishas*), to consult on a secret topic. So says the lizard," said Lakshmaṇakôn to Râmakôn, and at that very moment a light was seen at a distance. "It is the minister's carriage. Let us be off. God only must save the prince." So saying, they both ran away.

The feelings of the prince inside were like that of a man who was being led to the gallows. The bitterest enemy of his life, the minister himself, was coming to that very place where he was hiding. "I foolishly accused my old guardian, Raṇavîrasiṅg, and now I see his good intentions. How I am to be spared from this calamity Śaṅkara only knows." Thus thinking, he hurriedly fled to the inmost part of the temple behind the very image, and sat down there, still like a stump, without even breathing freely, lest his breath might reveal him. He had ample time there to admire the sound knowledge of the shepherds in interpreting the lizard chirps, their simplicity, their honesty and truthfulness; for, had they been otherwise, they might at once have caught hold of the prince and made him over to the tiger minister. True to the interpretation of the second shepherd, a carriage stopped in front of the Gaṇêśa temple, and there came out of it the Mantrî and the Pradhânî. Excepting themselves and, of course, the carriage driver and, as we know, the prince behind the Gaṇêśa, there were no others there. Kharavadana and his subordinate chose that solitary place at the dead of night to hold secret consultations. The Mantrî spoke first, and one could easily perceive from his words that he was in a fit of anger. "Why should the prince be thus allowed to ride free through my streets? Of the innumerable servants who eat our salt was there not one to cut down that impertinent head?" roared the minister. The Pradhânî replied, "My king, my lord, excuse me first for the humble words that I am going to speak before your honour. We have taken up a kingdom to which we have no right. If the prince had demanded the throne two years ago, we ought rightfully to have returned it to him. He never asked, and we did not restore it. He never troubles us with demands, but lives like a poor subject of the crown in his own quarters. Such being the case, why should we kill him? Why should we murder

[35] Minister.

[36] The chief officer of the realm next to the minister.

the only son of our old and much-respected king Śivâchâr? What I beg to suggest to your honour is, that we should no more trouble ourselves about his poor head." The Pradhânî, as he discovered that these words were not to the taste of Kharavadana, stopped at once without proceeding further, though he had much to say upon that subject. "Vile wretch! Dare you preach morals to your superiors. You shall see the result of this, before the morning dawns," bawled out the Minister. The Pradhânî saw that all his excellent advice was like blowing a horn in a deaf man's ears. He feared for his own life, and so at once begged a thousand pardons, and promised to bring the head of the prince within a week. And as Kharavadana wanted only that, he spared the Pradhânî. They then talked on different subjects, and prepared to start.

The prince inside, behind the Gaṇêśavigraha,[37] was now almost stifled to death. The short breaths that he inhaled and exhaled were themselves enough to kill him. Add to that the horrible words that fell on his ears. For all that he continued to hide himself. Kharavadana and the Pradhânî finished their conversation and got into the carriage. Sundara called courage to his assistance, "Śaṅkara has saved me till now; he may so save me throughout." So thinking to himself, he boldly came out of the temple without making the least noise and sat behind the carriage, and, as it rolled on, thought again within himself: "I will follow these, come what may, and find out what more plans they devise against my life."

The carriage drove on to the opposite end of the town. It passed the west gate and entered a big park outside the town. The undaunted prince followed. In the middle of the park a fine tank was discovered. The banks looked like day, being lighted up profusely. In the midst of the tank a small island with a gaudy mansion was seen. Pillars of gold, sofas of silver and doors of diamonds made it the very *Indralôka*[38] itself. A broad road with avenues of sweet smelling flowering trees connected the island with the bank. It was at that road that the carriage stopped. The prince, before that was reached, had got down and hid himself under the shade of a tree, to see unobserved all that passed in the mansion which he had every reason to believe was the destination of the minister. Kharavadana descended from the carriage and sent the Pradhânî home. What most astonished the prince was the absence of male servants in that garden. At the entrance of the road twenty young females of the most exquisite beauty waited and conducted Kharavadana through the sweet bower to the mansion. When it was reached, the minister sat down on a most richly furnished gold couch, and ordered the females there to bring the queen. Ten females arranged themselves on each side of an ivory palanquin, and started, apparently, to bring the queen in it. "These females themselves resemble Rambhâ,[39] Urvaśî,[40] &c. A woman who has beauty superior to the heads of these females must, of course, be of the greatest beauty imaginable in this world. Let me see her." Thus thinking, the prince Sundara anxiously awaited the return of the palanquin. In a few minutes it came. A female of the most charming beauty jumped briskly out of it. The minister came running to give his helping hand to her. Horror

[37] The image of the belly-god.

[38] The world of Indra, the regent of the sky.

[39] Names of divine damsels.

[40] Names of divine damsels.

of horrors, what sees the prince! It was his own wife, the very girl that the minister had married to him a few years before, that got down from the palanquin. "Are my eyes deceived? Do they perform their functions aright? Let me look once more." So again and again wiping his eyes to clear them a little, the prince saw distinctly. It was his very wife herself. "Oh, I most foolishly accused that grey-headed guardian for a wicked fool, because he would not allow me to be friends with my wife. I now see what he saw a long time ago. Perhaps if I had seen more of her I should have thus been brought in here by some secret way that these devils seem now to have to the inmost parts of the palace. If I had taken anything from her hands I should have died that very day. My poor old man, my Raṇavîrasiṅg it is, who has saved me from all these calamities." These thoughts and a thousand more were passing through Sundara's mind when he saw his wife sitting down on the same couch with the minister. She accused him of the delay in murdering her husband, of his letting all opportunities escape during the morning ride. "Horrible! Did you, Kharavadana, marry me to such a faithful wife! Thank God and Raṇavîrasiṅg that I have not fallen into her snares," thought Sundara to himself. The minister offered a thousand excuses, related to her all that had taken place between himself and the Pradhânî, and of what the latter had promised. Then they both retired to bed. At that moment the treacherous owl began to hoot, and one of the maid-servants, who happened to be a clever interpreter of owl-hootings revealed, to secure the favour of the minister, that the prince was lurking behind a tree in that very garden. Knowing the price set on Sundara's head even female hands flew to cut it off. All ran with torches to search the garden.

These words, of course, fell upon the ears of the prince like thunder. Before the people there began their search he began his race, jumped over a high wall, and flew like a kite. Before the lady-racers and the minister had left their sweet road to the tank-bank, Sundara found himself in the north street of the town. The news that the prince was out that night spread like a flame from the pleasure-park outside throughout the whole town, and before long avaricious persons were searching in the streets for his valuable head. Sundara thought it dangerous to pass through the streets, and wished to hide himself in a safe place. Fortune conducted him to one. It was a ruined old choultry, where food, during the days of his father, was distributed in charity to the beggars of the town, and which was now only resorted to by them to sleep, and not to receive rice. The prince entered it, and laid himself down in the midst of them, fortunately unobserved. He could hear from where he was the noise of the persons searching outside. In the garden the minister searched in vain, and accusing the female for her wrong interpretation as he thought, retired to bed.

Outside the north gate, at a distance of three *ghaṭikâs'* walk, lived a robber. He used to start out on a plundering expedition once in seven years. In the houses and mansions he used to rob he took only jewels of various kinds, *Gômêda,*[41] *pushparûga,* (topaz) *vajra,*[42] *vaiḍûrya,*[43] &c.; gold and silver he rejected as being too mean for his dignity. As he was a high-caste robber, he used to take a coolie with him

[41] Cinnamon-stone.

[42] Diamond.

[43] A precious stone (cat's eye).

on his way to carry his booty. Of course, that coolie never returned from the cave. He was put to death after his services were over, lest he should disclose the secret of the robber.

Unfortunately, that new-moon night happened to be the night of that cruel robber's plundering expedition. He came out, and when he saw people in search of the prince, thinking that he was not in his palace, he wanted to plunder it. Wishing for a coolie, he entered the ruined choultry, to pick out one among the beggars there. Passing over the others he came to the prince. He found him stout and strong. "This beggar will do me good service to-day. I shall break my custom, and amply reward this man for his services." So thinking to himself, the gentleman robber tapped Sundara with his cane on the back. The prince had just closed his eyes. In the short sleep that ensued he dreamt that the minister's servants were pursuing him, and that one had caught him. At that very moment the gentleman-robber's stroke fell upon his back, giving a sort of reality to his dream. He awoke with horror. "Tell me who you are," asked the unknown person, "A beggar," was the reply. "How does the night appear to you?" asked the robber. "As dark as dark can be," replied the prince. The robber applied a sort of *kajjala*[44] to the prince's eyes, and asked, "How does the night appear now?" "As luminous as if a *karôṛ* of suns were in the sky," answered Sundara. The robber applied a *tilaka*[45] to the intended coolie's forehead and addressed him thus: "I am a robber, now going to plunder the palace, from which the prince is absent. Follow me. I shall reward you richly. The *kajjala* has made the night a day to you. The *tilaka* takes you unobserved wherever you wish to go." So saying, and dragging the coolie or supposed coolie by the hand, the robber went off to the palace. Wherever he found a door locked, he applied a leaf that he carried in his hand to the fastening, and behold, the lock flew back, and the door opened of its own accord. The prince was astonished. In a few minutes the robber opened one and all of the gates and boxes, and extracted all the precious stones. He tied them up in a bundle, and set it on the prince's head, and asked him to follow. Sundara followed. He assisted in the plunder of his own palace, and carried the booty behind the robber, who, praised be his stupidity, never for one moment suspected he was a prince, but admired his coolie for the beauty of his person, thought of saving his life, and also of making him his son-in-law. For the robber had a beautiful daughter, for whom he had long been searching for a suitable husband. So with this thought he reached the cave, stopped before it, and taking the bundle from the prince's head ordered him to go into a large cell, the mouth of which he covered with a big stone, which he lifted up by pronouncing an incantation over it. The robber went with the bundle to his wife, and described to her the beauty of the coolie, and what a fair match he would be for their daughter. The wife did not like it, and asked her husband to do with the coolie as they usually did, *i.e.*, murder him; and the robber, who never in anything acted against the will of his wife, went in to fetch his weapon.

Meanwhile the robber's daughter, an excellent girl, of the most charming beauty, overhearing all that took place between her parents, came running to the cave where the coolie was confined. She pronounced a single word over the stone

[44] A sort of paint for the eye (*Hindustani*—Surmâ).

[45] A mark on the forehead.

lid of the cave, and it opened, and the prince, who had lost all hopes of recovery, now beheld a beautiful girl coming towards him. "Whoever you may be, my dear coolie, fly for your life for the present. You are my husband. My father has so named you, but as my mother does not like it, he has gone to fetch his weapon to murder you. Excepting we three, none, not even Brahmâ, can open the once-shut gates. After hearing you once called my husband, I must ever regard you so. Now fly, and escape my father's sharp sword. If you are a man, marry me in kind remembrance of the assistance rendered. If you fail to do so you are a beast, and I shall die a virgin." So saying she conducted out in haste the supposed coolie, who had only time to take a hasty embrace, whispering in her ear that he was the prince, and that he would marry her without fail. He now ran for his life. Fearing the robber would come after him he left the way by which he reached the cave, and passing through unknown fields reached the south gate of the town. By that time the search for him had almost abated, and the prince, praising God for his delivery, reached the south street. The night was almost spent. Before returning to the palace he wished to take rest for a few minutes, till he had recovered his breath, and so he sat down on the pyal of an old and almost ruined house.

That happened to be the house of a poor Brâhmaṇ, who had not even sufficient clothes to wear. As the prince sat down in a corner of the pyal the door of the house opened, and the old Brâhmaṇ came out. The old woman, the Brâhmaṇî, was standing at the door with a vessel containing water for her husband. Śubhâśâstrî, for that was the Brâhmaṇ's name, looked up to the sky for a couple of minutes, after which he heaved a deep sigh, and said, "Alas, the prince, the only son of our former protector, Śivâchâr, is not to remain for more than two *ghaṭikâs*. A *kâlasarpa* (black serpent) will sting him. What shall we do? We are poor. If we could begin *Sarpahôma*[46] now we could tie the mouth of the snake, sacrifice it in the fire, and thus save the prince." So saying the poor Brâhmaṇ cried. Sundara, who overheard everything, jumped down in confusion, and fell at the feet of the Brâhmaṇ, who asked him who he was. "I am a herdsman of the palace. Preserve my master's life," was the reply. Śubhâśâstrî was extremely poor. He had no means to procure a small quantity of *ghî* even to begin the *hôma*.[47] He did not know what to do. He begged from his neighbours, who all laughed at his stupidity, and ridiculed his astrology. The prince in a hopeless state of anguish wrung his hands, and in wringing them he felt his ring. Drawing it off his finger he gave it to Śubhâśâstrî, and requested him to pawn it. The latter resorted to the nearest bâzâr, and awakening the bâzâr-keeper procured from him a little *ghî*, by pawning the ring. Running home and bathing in cold water the Brâhmaṇ sat down for the *hôma*. The prince, fearing the serpent, wished to sit inside the house, but at a distance from the place of the ceremony. Just at the appointed hour a large black serpent broke through the sky, fell on the head of the prince, whom he was not able to bite, and gave up its life in the fire. "This is no shepherd, but the very prince himself," said the Brâhmaṇî.[48] Sundara rose up, and running surrounded them thrice, spoke to them thus:—"You alone are my parents and protectors. This night has been a most adventurous one

[46] Serpent sacrifice.

[47] Sacrifice.

[48] Brâhmaṇ woman.

with me. There was every possibility of my escaping every other calamity, and so I did. But no other power except yours could have averted this snake-bite. So my rescue is due to you alone. I have no time to lose now. Before daylight I must fly unobserved to the palace, and you shall before long see my reward for this." So saying, Sundara ran to his palace and entered.

Raṇavîrasiṅg was almost dead. The rumour that the prince was out reached him. He was astonished at the way in which Sundara had got out. He searched the whole palace. To his astonishment all the rooms had previously been opened and plundered. "Has the prince been stolen away by some vile tricks from the palace," thought Raṇavîrasiṅg, and without knowing what to do he was buried in the ocean of sorrow, from which he gave up all hopes of recovering. What was his joy, then, when he saw the prince enter the palace just at dawn. "*Mai Bâb Chakravarti,* where have you been the whole night, throwing away the advice of your poor slave? How many enemies you have in this world, you have yet to know," said Raṇavîrasiṅg. "I know them all now, only listen to what I say, and do as I bid. I have won the crown without a blow. Thank the day that gave me you as my protector, for it was only yesterday that I had ample reason to verify your statements. My adventures would make your hair stand on end. Thank God I have escaped from all of them unhurt. If you have a few men ready now, we have won the kingdom." So saying, the prince explained to him every detail of his adventure. "If we catch hold of the minister now, we have done all." "I could never for one moment think that you in a single night could have seen and done so much. Now that heaven has shown you the way, I shall obey you," said Raṇavîrasiṅg, and Sundara accordingly issued the orders. He described the house with the pyal at which he had lingered for a while the previous night, and asked a servant to bring the owner of that house to the Râjasthânik office. Raṇavîrasiṅg brought in the Pradhânî, who was extremely delighted at the good intention of the prince. He was offered the Mantrî's place. Two were sent to the shepherds. Twenty were sent to the pleasure-park to have the minister and his sweet paramour brought to the court in chains. The female servants were also ordered to be brought. The robber and his cruel wife were not forgotten. The prince minutely described the cave, and asked his servants to catch and imprison the robber by surprising him suddenly, without giving him time to have recourse to his vile tricks—lock-breaking *kajjala,* &c. The palace palanquin was sent for the robber's daughter, whom the prince had firmly made up his mind to marry. The palace elephants were decked and sent to fetch with all pomp Śubhâśâstrî and his wife to the court. Thus, without a single stroke, Sundara won the kingdom. Raṇavîrasiṅg was thunder-struck by the excellent and bold way in which the prince in one night went through the series of calamities, and successfully overcame them all. The Pradhânî's delight knew no bounds. He himself broke open the court and every one connected with the previous night's adventure was ushered in. The prince bathed, offered up his prayers, and attended the council. When Śubhâśâstrî came in with his wife the prince put them on the *simhâsana,*[49] and himself standing before them, explained to all his previous night's adventures, rewarded the poor Brâhmaṇ and the shepherds, punished by banishment the maid-servant who, knowing that the prince's

[49] Throne.

head was coveted, revealed his concealment, and ordered his wife, the minister, the robber, and the robber's wife to be beheaded. He rewarded without limit his protector, Śubhâśâstrî, and married the robber's daughter, being won over by her sincerity. The Pradhânî, as we have said already, he made his minister, and with his old guardian, the faithful Raṇavîrasiṅg, the prince reigned for several years in the kingdom of Vañjaimânagar.

# CHAPTER V.

## "CHARITY ALONE CONQUERS."

### *Dharmamê jayam.*

In the town of Têvai[50] there lived a king called Suguṇa. He had an excellent minister named Dharmaśîla. They ruled for a long time in prosperity over the kingdom. Both of them had sons. The prince's name was Subuddhi. He was a noble prince, and quite in keeping with his name, was always bent upon doing good to the world. The minister's son was named Durbuddhi, a most wicked boy, whose only delight was teasing beasts and birds from his infancy, and which ripened into all sorts of wickedness as he grew to boyhood. Notwithstanding the difference between their temperaments the prince and the minister's son were the best of friends. The motto of the prince was *Dharmamê jayam*—Charity alone conquers. That of the minister's son was *Adharmamê jayam*—Absence of Charity alone conquers. When rising from their beds, when beginning their prayers, when sitting down for meals or study, and, in fact, before beginning to do anything, each repeated his motto. The people had great hopes in Subuddhi, whom they fully expected to see a good and benevolent king; but the minister's son all thoroughly hated. Even the minister himself, his father, hated his son for his vile turn of mind, which he found impossible to change. His only friend, as we have already said, was the prince, who, notwithstanding all his faults, loved him sincerely. Both of them had grown up together from their very cradle, had played in the same dust, had read their lessons side by side in the same school under the same teachers. Fortune so ordained that the prince's mind should take such a bent, while the mind of the minister's son turned in a crooked way.

Nor was Durbuddhi insensible to the disgust and dislike which every one manifested towards him. He was well aware of all that was going on around. Still he would not change.

"I have no friend in this world excepting yourself, my dear Subuddhi," exclaimed Durbuddhi one day to his royal friend while they were riding together.

"Fear nothing. I shall ever stand by you as your true friend," replied Subuddhi.

"My very father hates me. Who else would like me then? On the other hand, every one likes you. You may soon get yourself married to some beautiful lady, while I must remain a bachelor; for no girl would marry me. You may soon rise to

[50] Têvai is the classical name of the modern town of Râmnâd in the district of Madurâ.

the place of a king; but I cannot become your minister, as the people do not like me. What can I do?" So said the minister's son, and hung down his head, as if conscious for a time of the utter hatred with which the people regarded him.

Subuddhi replied, "Heed it not, I will make you my minister, give you everything you want, and see you well provided for."

"If so, will you give me your wife one day, at least, if you happen to get married before me, and if I remain a bachelor after you," were the words which the wretched Durbuddhi shamelessly uttered to the face of his only friend.

These words were enough in themselves to enrage the prince's mind. But he was of so good a nature that instead of becoming angry, he smiled at the stupidity of his companion, and agreed that he would thus give him his wife one day in case he got married first. Thus took place an agreement between Subuddhi and Durbuddhi while they were still quite young.

Several years passed after this agreement, when one day the prince went to hunt in a neighbouring forest. His inseparable companion, the minister's son, and several hunters followed him to the wood. The prince and the minister's son both gave chase to a deer. They rode so much in advance of the hunters that they lost themselves in a thick jungle, where the latter could neither see nor follow them. The hunters returned after dark, and informed the king and the minister about the disappearance of their sons. They thought that as their sons were grown-up men they need not fear for their safety.

The two friends chased the deer and found themselves in the midst of a thick forest in the evening. Except a slight breakfast in the early morning they had tasted no other food. Hunger was pinching them severely. The hot chase had awakened a severe thirst, to quench which they were not able to find a drop of water. In utter hopelessness of life they resigned themselves to the course of their steeds. The beasts seemed very well to understand the wants of their royal riders. They went on trotting, and at last, about midnight, stopped on the banks of a large tank.

The riders, who were almost dead with thirst, opened their closed eyes when the horses stopped. All of a sudden, and to their great joy, they found themselves on the banks of a large tank. Their joy knew no bounds.

"Surely God takes care of His children. Had it not been for His kind care how could we have come to this tank, when we had given ourselves up to the guidance of our horses?" thought Subuddhi to himself, and got down from his horse.

The minister's son, who had become more exhausted by that time than his companion, also alighted. Subuddhi, true to the nobility of his mind, took both the steeds first to water, and, after satisfying their thirst and loosening them to graze by the side of a grassy meadow, he went into the water to quench his thirst. The minister's son also followed. After a short prayer Subuddhi took some handfuls of water, and returned to the bank. Durbuddhi also returned. They chose a clean spot, and sat down to rest during the remaining part of the night. The prince, when taking his seat, pronounced his usual motto, "Charity alone conquers," and the minister's son also repeated his, "Absence of Charity alone conquers."

These words fell like venom into the ears of the prince at that time. He could not control his anger then, notwithstanding his mild disposition. The hardships of the day, their fortunate arrival on a tank in the dead of night to have their thirst quenched, were fresh in Subuddhi's mind, and the prayers that he was offering to God were not yet over. That the minister's son should never think of all this, and go on with his own stupid motto even at that time was intolerable to Subuddhi.

"Vile wretch! detested atheist! have you no shame, to utter your wicked motto even after such calamities? It is not too late even now. Mend your character. Think of the God that saved you just now. Believe in Him. Change your motto from this day." Thus spoke the angry prince to the minister's son.

Durbuddhi, who was naturally of a wicked and quarrelsome temperament, flew into a rage at once at the excellent advice of the prince.

"Stop your mouth. I know as well as you do; you cannot wag your tail here. I can oppose you single-handed in this forest."

Thus saying, the minister's son sprang like an enraged lion at Subuddhi, who, as he never dreamt of any such thing, was completely overpowered by the wicked Durbuddhi. The prince was thrown down in the twinkling of an eye, and the minister's son was upon him. He severely thrashed his royal master, and, taking hold of a twig that was lying close by, tore out the prince's two eyes, filled up the sockets with sand, and ran away with his horse, thinking that he had completely killed him.

Subuddhi was almost dead; his body was bruised all over; his eyes were no more; his physical pain was unbearable.

"Is there a God over us all?" thought Subuddhi. The night was almost over. The cool and sweet breeze of the morning gave him some strength. He rose up, and, crawling on the ground, felt his way to the entrance of a temple. He crept in, shut the gates, and fastened the bolt.

It happened to be a temple of the fierce *Kâlî*. She used to go out every morning to gather roots and fruits, and to return at evening. That day, when she returned, she found her gates shut against her. She threatened with destruction the usurper of her temple. A voice, and we know that it was Subuddhi's, replied from within:

"I am already dying of the loss of my eyes. So, if in anger you kill me, it is so much the better; for what use is there in my living blind? If, on the contrary, you pity me, and by your divine power give me my eyes, I shall open the gates."

Kâlî was in a very difficult position. She was very hungry, and saw no other way of going inside than by giving Subuddhi his eyes.

"Open the gates; your request is granted," said Kâlî. No sooner were these words uttered than the prince recovered his eyes. His delight may be better imagined than described. He opened the gates and vowed before Kâlî that he would from that day continue in that temple as her servant and worshipper.

The wretched Durbuddhi, after his horrible act, rode on composedly, following the footsteps of his horse, and reached the forest where he had been hunting the day before in company with the prince. He thence returned home all alone. When his father saw him coming back he suspected something wrong to the prince, and asked his son what had become of him.

"We chased a deer, and he rode so much in advance of me that he was out of sight, and finding all search vain, I returned alone," was Durbuddhi's reply.

"This I would have believed from anyone but yourself. Never plant your feet in these dominions till you bring back the prince again. Run for your life," was the order of the minister, and Durbuddhi accordingly ran off, fearing the anger of his father.

Thus the Prince Subuddhi served in the Kâlî temple; and Durbuddhi, fully confident that he had killed his friend, roamed about from place to place, as he saw no possibility of returning to his own country without the prince.

Thus passed several months. The goddess Kâlî was extremely delighted at the sincere devotion of Subuddhi, and, calling him one day to her side, said:

"My son! I am delighted with your great devotion to me. Enough of your menial services here. Better return now to your kingdom. Your parents are likely to be much vexed at your loss. Go and console their minds." Thus ended Kâlî, and Subuddhi replied:

"Excuse me, my goddess, my mother, I no more regard them as my parents. This wood is not a large place if they wished to search for me. As they were so careless about me, I shall also from this day disregard them. You are my father and mother. Therefore permit me to end my days here in your service." So saying, Subuddhi begged Kâlî to allow him to stay, and the goddess agreed accordingly, for some time at least.

After a few more months, Kâlî called the prince again to her, and addressed him thus:

"My boy! I have devised another plan. Better not, then, go to your parents, as you do not wish to go now. At a short distance from this place, in the Kâvêrî country, reigns a staunch devotee of mine. His daughter had small-pox, and as he forgot to do proper respect to me, I have blinded both her eyes. The king has issued a proclamation that he will give the whole kingdom and his daughter in marriage to him who would cure her of her defect. He has hung up a bell (*ghaṇṭâ*) at which every physician who wishes to try the case strikes. The king comes running as soon as he hears the sound, takes home the doctor and shows him the case. Several persons have tried in vain; for who could repair a defect inflicted by the displeasure of the gods? Now I mean to send you there. That king is a staunch worshipper of my feet. Though I have punished him, still I pity the sad calamity that has come upon his daughter. You had better go there and strike the bell. He will take you and show you the case. For three consecutive days apply my holy ashes to her eyes. Though fools may deride these ashes, still by them a true devotee can work wonders. On the fourth day her eyes will be perfectly restored. Then you will secure her hand, and, what is more, the country of Kâvêrî. Reign there, for you are born to reign, being a prince, and not to spend your time here in this wood. If you do not do so you will commit a sin, and, what is more, incur my displeasure."

Thus ended Kâlî, and the prince could not refuse; for he feared the anger of the goddess. Agreeing to her words, and with her manifold blessings, he started and reached the kingdom of Kâvêrî.

He struck the bell. The king came running to welcome the new doctor. All the previous physicians had tried by medicines external and internal. The new doctor—Prince Subuddhi—proposed to treat the case by *mantras*—incantations. The old king, who was very religious, fully believed that the new doctor might effect the cure, and, just as he expected, on the fourth day his daughter's sight was completely restored. The king's joy knew no bounds. He enquired into the parentage of the doctor: and when he came to know that he had princely blood in his veins, that he was as honourably descended as himself, his joy was greatly increased. He sent up a thousand prayers to the god for giving him a royal son-in-law. As promised in his notice, he would have to give his daughter to anyone, whatever he might be, who effected the cure. The lowest beggar, the lowest caste-man, if he had only succeeded in curing her, would have had as much claim to her hand as the prince-physician. So when the person that effected the cure proved to be a prince, the king was extremely delighted, and at once made all arrangements for the marriage of his daughter, and gave her to Subuddhi: and, himself being very old, he gave the kingdom also to the prince at the same time.

Thus by the favour of Kâlî, Subuddhi had a princess for his wife and a kingdom to govern. Subuddhi, as we know, was an excellent man. Though he became king now, he consulted his father-in-law in all matters, and, in fact, acted only as manager for the old man. Every evening he used to consult him for an hour or two before disposing of intricate cases. The duty of signing, too, he reserved for the old man. Thus even on those days when there were no cases he used to go to his father-in-law to get papers signed. Thus passed on a couple of years or so.

One evening, while sitting in company with his wife in the loftiest room of his palace after the duties of the day, he cast his eyes to the east main street and contemplated the bustle of that part of the town. Carts creaking under the load of merchandise, the flourish with which the goods and wares were exposed for sale, fashionable gentlemen in their fanciful evening costumes walking to and fro, the troublesome hawkers that stand by the roadside questioning every one as to what they would buy, and several other things interested him, and for a time made him somewhat proud even, that he ruled over such a rich country. But sweetness is not always unaccompanied with bitterness. He saw in that same street a man whose face was very familiar to him, but whom he could not at once make out. A black man was sitting on a projecting pyal of a corner of a shop, and was mending some torn gunny bags. Subuddhi looked at him carefully.

"Is it the minister's son, Durbuddhi? No; he is not so black; rather was not when I saw him last," thought Subuddhi with himself, and examining his face, he at last exclaimed, "It is he! It is he! It is my friend and companion." "Who is it?" exclaimed the princess, and rushed at once to his side. She had most carefully watched her husband's face for the past few minutes while he was in deep contemplation. "It is my friend, the minister's son, by name Durbuddhi. We were companions from our birth; we played in the same dust, read in the same school, and were ever inseparable companions. I do not know what has brought him to the condition in which I see him now," said Subuddhi, and sent some one to fetch him. Of the wicked and base act of the vile Durbuddhi he did not care to inform his gentle wife, who now retired to her inner apartments, as decorum did not allow her to be in company with her husband when he was receiving others.

The persons sent brought in Durbuddhi. Whatever might have been the cruelty that he had received from the hands of the minister's son, the prince began to shed tears when he saw his old companion ushered in, not in that blooming cheerful red complexion in which he had seen him last, but in a weather-beaten dark skin and dejected colour of a coolie in which he saw him a few minutes ago.

"I excuse you all your faults, my dear Durbuddhi. Tell me quickly what has brought you to this wretched plight," asked Subuddhi, and while asking he began to cry aloud. The minister's son also shed tears copiously, and cried or pretended to cry; for be it known that he was a perfect scoundrel, born to no good in the world.

"My own mischief has brought me to this plight. When I returned to our country, after putting out your eyes and thinking that I had killed you, my father banished me from our dominions, and ordered me never to plant my feet within their limits without bringing you back. As I thought I had put an end to your life I never came back to that tank in search of you. I engaged myself as a coolie in the streets of this town after trying several other places without success, and I now stand before you." Thus ended Durbuddhi, and the prince quite forgot his cruelty to him. He ordered his servants to get the minister's son bathed, and attired in as rich robes as he himself wore. Then he related to him his own story, without omitting a single point, and at once made him his minister.

The whole story of Durbuddhi, excepting the single point of his having put out his eyes, the prince related to his wife, father, and mother-in-law.

Thus was Durbuddhi again restored to his high position, through the liberal kindness of Subuddhi. Subuddhi did not stop even at this. He began to send him with papers and other things to the old king for signature. This went on for some months. All the while Durbuddhi was as obedient as might be, and by his vile tricks had completely won over the heart of the old king.

One evening, after the signatures were over, Durbuddhi stopped for a while as if desirous to speak. "What do you want?" said the old king. "Nothing but your favour," was the only reply, after which he retired. Thus he went on for some days and weeks. Every day he stopped for a few minutes after the state business was over, and when the old king asked the reason for it went on giving evasive answers. At last one evening the old king was extremely provoked. The cunning Durbuddhi had purposely intended this.

"What a big fool are you to stop every day as if wishing to speak and never to utter a word," broke out the old king.

"I beg pardon of your honour; I was thinking all the while whether I should let out my secret or not. At last, I have come to the conclusion that I will keep it to myself," replied the diabolical Durbuddhi.

"No, you shall let it out," roared the old king, whose curiosity was more roused than abated by the words, purposely obscure, of the minister's son. Durbuddhi, after simulating much reluctance at disclosing the supposed secret, loudly began his harangue:

"My lord, ever since I came here I have been making enquiries about the nobility of your family, about the sacrifices that you and your ancestors have performed, about the purifications that you and your elders have undergone, and about a thousand other particulars, each of which is enough to secure you and your descendants the place of Achyuta (*Achyutapada*) himself. These delighted me for a time—I say for a time—for listen, please, to what follows. When I compared with the pure fame of your famous family, that of your son-in-law, my heart began to pain me. Indeed the pain which began at that moment has not yet ceased. Know, then, that your son-in-law is not a prince. No doubt he has royal blood in his veins, which makes him look like a king. How came he to be so skilful in medicine. Just enquire the cause. To be no more in the dark, the king of my country—over which my father is the minister—set out one day on *savâr*. While passing a barber's street he saw a beautiful damsel of that caste. Bewitched by her beauty the king wanted to include her in his harem, notwithstanding her low position in society. The child of that woman, is your son-in-law. He being the son of a barber-mother acquired thus easily the art of medicine. That a king was his father makes him look like a prince. If he had been of pure birth why should he leave his kingdom, and come here to effect the cure of your daughter? Except this prince, or supposed prince, all those that came here were mere doctors by caste." Thus ended the vile Durbuddhi, and taking in his hand the papers, vanished out of the room quickly, like a serpent that had stung.

The sweet words in which the minister's son clothed his arguments, the rising passion at the thought that he had been falsely imposed upon by a barber's son, the shame—or rather supposed shame—that he thought had come over his family, and a thousand other feelings clouded for a time the clear reason of the old king. He saw no other way of putting an end to the shame than by the murder of his dear daughter and son-in-law first, and of his own self and queen afterwards. At once he sent for the executioner, who came in. He gave him his signet-ring, and commanded him to break open the bed-room of his son-in-law that midnight, and murder him with his wife while asleep. The *hukums*, or orders given with signet-rings, can never be disobeyed. The executioner humbled himself to the ground, as a sign of his accepting the order, and retired to sharpen his knife for his terrible duty.

Neither Subuddhi nor his affectionate wife had any reason to suspect this terrible mandate. The old queen and the treacherous Durbuddhi had equally no reason to know anything about it. The old man, after issuing the *hukum*, shut himself up in his closet, and began to weep and wail as if he had lost his daughter from that moment. Durbuddhi, after kindling the fire, as says the Tamil proverb, by means of his treachery, came back with the papers to the prince. A thought occurred in his mind that Subuddhi's fate was drawing near. He wanted to carry out the agreement between himself and the prince about the latter's wife. The excellent Subuddhi, who always observed oaths most strictly, was confused for a time. He did not know what to do. To stick to the oath and surrender his wife to another; or to break it and preserve the chastity of his own wife. At last, repeating in his own mind, "Charity alone conquers," and also thinking that Heaven would somehow devise to preserve his wife, he went to her, explained to her how the matter stood, and ordered her to go to the minister's son. She hesitatingly consented; for, as a good wife, she could not disobey her husband's commands. Subuddhi then told Durbuddhi that he might have his wife as his own.

The princess went to her mother, crying that her husband had turned out mad. "Or else who would promise to give his wife to another. What does he mean by that?"

"My daughter! fear nothing, perhaps, in his boyhood, he made this rash promise without thinking. The promise once made now pains him. Unable to break it, and leaving it to yourself to preserve your chastity, he has so ordered you. And he would, nay must, excuse you, if you by some means or other save yourself, and apparently make good your husband's promise also. A thought just comes to me how to do that. There is your foster-sister, exactly resembling you. I shall send her in your place." So consoling her daughter, the old queen at once made all the requisite arrangements. And, of course, Subuddhi had no reason then to know anything about them.

In the middle of the night his door is forced open, and a ruffian with a drawn sword, blazing like lightning, rushes in, and murders the pair. Thus in that very night in which Durbuddhi had reached the topmost point of his vice, he was cut down by the supreme hand of God. For, it is said, that when crime increases, God himself cannot tolerate it.

The morning dawned. Subuddhi rose from his couch, and after his morning prayers was sitting in the council hall. The princess and her mother rose from their beds, and were attending to their business. A servant just at that time came running to the old queen, and said:

"Our king is weeping in his room that his daughter is now no more. I think that there is something wrong with his majesty's brains to-day. Come and console him."

The queen, who knew nothing of what had happened, ran to her husband's room, quite astonished at the change. The husband reported everything to her—the sage-looking minister's son, the barber's son-in-law, and everything, and then concluded that their daughter and son-in-law were no more.

"What! compose yourself. Our son-in-law is sitting in his durbar. Our daughter is just adorning herself in her dressing-room. Were you dreaming? Are you in your right senses?" said the queen.

The king ordered the executioner to bring the heads, which, on examination, proved to be those of the minister's son and of the foster-sister. The queen told everything of the one-day-wife-giving engagement, and her own arrangements about it. The old king could not understand what all this meant. He drew out his sword and ran to the durbar like a maddened lion, and stood armed before his son-in-law.

"Relate to me your true origin, and everything respecting yourself. Speak the truth. How came you to learn medicine? If you are a prince why should you leave your own dominions and come down here? What about this wicked agreement of giving your wife to another? Who is this minister's son?"

Subuddhi, without omitting a single point, related everything that had taken place, even to the putting out of his eyes. The old man threw down his sword, took his son-in-law in his arms almost, for so great was his joy at the excellent way which fate had prepared for his escape, and said:

"My son, my life, my eye. True it is, true it is. *Dharma* alone conquers, and you that hold that motto have conquered everything. The vile wretch whom, notwithstanding the series of rogueries that he practised upon you, you protected, has at last found out that his *Adharmam* never conquers. But he never found it out. It was his *Adharmam* that cut him off on the very night of his supposed complete conquest by it."

Letters were sent at once to Têvai, inviting Suguṇa and Dharmaśîla to the happy rejoicings at the prince and princess's delivery, and a re-marriage was celebrated with all pomp, in honour of their lucky escape. Dharmaśîla, as he disliked his son, never shed a single tear for his loss. Subuddhi lived for a long time, giving much consolation to his own and his wife's parents. Through the blessings of Kâlî they had several intelligent sons.

# CHAPTER VI.

## VIDÂMUNDAN KODÂMUNDAN.

## MR. WON'T-GIVE AND MR. WON'T-LEAVE.

In a certain town there lived a clever old Brâhmaṇ, named Won't-Give.[51] He used to go out daily and to beg in all the houses round, under the pretence that he had to feed several Brâhmaṇs in his own house. Good people, that believed in his words, used to give him much rice and curry stuffs, with which he would come home, and explain to his wife how he had deceived such and such a gentleman by the imposition of feeding in charity many persons at home. But if any hungry Brâhmaṇ, who had heard of his empty boast of feeding Brâhmaṇs at home, came to him, he was sent away with some excuse or other. In this way Mr. Won't-Give brought home a basketful of rice and other necessaries every day, of which he only used a small portion for himself and his wife, and converted the remainder into money. And thus, by imposition and tricks, he managed to live well for several years.

In an adjoining village there lived another very clever Brâhmaṇ, named Won't-Leave.[52] Whenever he found any man reluctant and unwilling to give him anything that he begged of him, he would persist in bothering him until he had wrung from him a dole. This Mr. Won't-Leave, hearing of the charity of Mr. Won't-Give, and his benevolent feeding of Brâhmaṇs, came to see him one day, and requested him to give him a meal. Mr. Won't-Give told him that for that day ten Brâhmaṇs had already been settled, and that if he came the next day he would have his meal without fail. Mr. Won't-Leave agreed to this, and left him for that day. Mr. Won't-Give had, of course, told him the very lie he was accustomed to tell all that occasionally begged meals of him.

Now Mr. Won't-Leave was not so stupid as to be thus imposed upon. He stood before Mr. Won't-Give's door precisely at the appointed *ghaṭikâ* (hour) the next day, and reminded the master of the house of his promise. Mr. Won't-Give had never before been taken at his word, and determined to send away the impertinent guest by some stronger excuse than the first, and so he spoke to him thus:—

"Sir, I am very sorry to say that my wife fell ill last night of a strong fever, from which she has not yet recovered. Owing to this unforeseen accident I have had to postpone my charitable feedings (*samârâdhana*) till her recovery, so do not trouble me, please, for some days more."

[51] *Kodâmundan.*

[52] *Vidâmundan.*

Mr. Won't-Leave heard these words with an expression of sincere, or rather, seemingly sincere, sorrow in his face, and replied:—

"Respected sir, I am very sorry for the illness of the mistress of the house, but to give up charitable feeding of Brâhmaṇs on that account is a great sin. For the last ten years I have been studying the art of cooking, and can now cook for even several hundreds of Brâhmaṇs; so I can assist you now in preparing the necessaries for the *samârâdhana*."

Mr. Won't-Give could not refuse such a request, but he deceitfully determined in his mind to get Mr. Won't-Leave to cook for him, and then to drive him away without giving him his rice. And so he said:—

"Yes, that is a very good idea. I am much obliged to you for your kind suggestion. Come in; let us cook together."

So saying, the master of the house took Mr. Won't-Leave inside and they both went into the kitchen, while the mistress of the house, at the command of her husband, pretended to be ill.

Now Mr. Won't-Give was a good liver, and prepared, with the assistance of Mr. Won't-Leave, several good dishes. And then the difficulty was to drive the fellow out, for the long-maintained rule of never feeding a single Brâhmaṇ must not be broken that day. So, when the cooking was all over, the master of the house gave to Mr. Won't-Leave a *kâśu* (copper coin), and asked him to bring some leaves from the *bâzâr* (for plates), and he accordingly went. Mr. Won't-Give, meanwhile, came to his wife, and instructed her thus:—

"My dearest wife, I have spared you the trouble of cooking to-day. Would that we could get such stupid fools as this every day to cook for us! I have now sent him out to fetch us some leaves, and it won't look well if we shut our doors against him or drive him away; so we must make him go away of his own accord. A thought has just come into my mind as to how we can do it. As soon as he comes you shall commence to quarrel with me. I shall then come to you and beat you, or, rather, the ground near you, with both my hands, and you must continue your abuse and cries. The guest will find this very disgusting, and will leave us of his own accord."

Mr. Won't-Give had just finished when he saw Mr. Won't-Leave returning with the leaves. The wife, as pre-arranged, abused her husband right and left for his great imprudence and over-liberality in feeding the Brâhmaṇs. Said she:

"How are we to get on in the world if you thus empty the house of everything we have in feeding big-bellied Brâhmaṇs? Must you be so particular as to invite them, even when I am sick?" These, and a thousand similar expressions, were now launched at the husband's head. He pretended not to hear it for a time, but at last, apparently overcome by anger, he went in and with his hands gave successive blows on the floor. At every blow on the floor the wife cried out that she was being murdered, and that those who had mercy in their hearts should come to her rescue.

Mr. Won't-Leave, from the court-yard of the house, listened to what was taking place inside, but not wishing to interfere in a quarrel between husband and wife, left matters to take their own course, and got into the loft, where he hid himself, fearing that he would be summoned as a witness to the quarrel.

After a time Mr. Won't-Give came out of the room where he had been beating the floor, and to his joy he could not find the guest. He cautiously looked round him and saw no signs of Mr. Won't-Leave. Of course, having had no reason to think that his guest would be sitting in the loft, he did not look up there; and even if he had done so, he would not have found him, for he had hidden himself out of sight.

Mr. Won't-Give now carefully bolted the door, and his wife came out and changed her dirty cloth for a clean one. Said her husband to her:

"At last we have succeeded in driving him out; come, you too must be hungry; let us have our dinner together."

Two leaves were spread on the ground, and all the dishes were equally divided into them. Meanwhile Mr. Won't-Leave was watching all that took place below him and, being himself very hungry, was slyly watching for an opportunity to jump down. Mr. Won't-Give, gloating over his trickery, said to his wife:

"Well, my love, did I not beat you without hurting you?" to which she replied:

"Did I not continue to cry without shedding tears?" when suddenly there fell on their ears:

"And did I not come to have my dinner without going away?" and down jumped Mr. Won't-Leave, from the loft, and took his seat in front of the leaf spread by Mr. Won't-Give for his wife. And Mr. Won't-Give, though disappointed, was highly pleased at the cleverness of his guest.

This story is cited as the authority for three proverbs that have come into use in Tamil.

> *"Nôvâmal aḍitten."*
> *"Oyâmal aluden."*
> *"Pôkâmal vandên."*

which represent the exchanges of politeness between the husband, the wife, and the guest, quoted in the foregoing paragraphs.

# CHAPTER VII.

## VAYALVALLAN KAIYAVALLA.

## MR. MIGHTY-OF-HIS-MOUTH AND MR. MIGHTY-OF-HIS-HANDS.

In two adjoining villages there lived two famous men. The one was called Mr. Mighty-of-his-mouth[53]—one that could accomplish wonders with words alone. The other was called Mr. Mighty-of-his-hands[54]—one who could make no use of that glib instrument the tongue, but was able to bear burdens, cut wood, and perform other physical labour.

It so happened that they agreed to live together in the house of the Mr. Mighty-of-his-mouth, to try and see which of them was the superior. They accordingly kept company for several months, till the great feast of the nine nights (*navarâtrî*) came on. On the first day of the feast Mr. Mighty-of-his-hands wanted to sacrifice a goat to the goddess Kâlî. So he said to Mr. Mighty-of-his-mouth,

"My dear friend, we both are mighty in our way, and so it would be shameful for us to buy the goat, that we want to sacrifice, with money. We should manage to get it without payment."

"Yes, we must do so, and I know how," replied Mr. Mighty-of-his-mouth, and he asked his friend to wait till that evening.

Now there lived a shepherd at one *ghaṭikâ's* (hour's) distance from their house, and the two friends resolved to go to his fold that night and steal away one of his goats. Accordingly, when it was dark, they approached his fold. The shepherd had just finished his duties to the mute members of his flock, and wanted to go home and have his rice hot. But he had no second person to watch the flock, and he must not lose his supper. So he planted his crook before the fold, and throwing his blanket (*kambalî*) over it, thus addressed it:

"My son, I am very hungry, and so must go for my rice. Till I return do you watch the flock. This wood is rich in tigers and goblins (*bhûtas*). Some mischievous thief or *bhûta*—or *kûta*[55] may come to steal away the sheep. Watch over them carefully." So saying the shepherd went away.

---

[53] *Vâyâlvallan.*

[54] *Kaiyâlvallan.*

[55] There is no such word as *kûta* in Tamil. The Tamil and other Dravidian languages allow rhyming repetitions of word, like this—*bhûta-kûta.*

The friends had heard what the shepherd said. Of course, Mr. Mighty-of-his-mouth laughed within himself at this device of the shepherd to impress upon would-be robbers that he had left some one there to watch his sheep, while really he had only planted a pole and thrown a blanket over it. Mr. Mighty-of-his-hands, however, did not see the trick, and mistaking the stick to be an actual watchman sitting at his duty before the fold, spoke thus to his friend:

"Now what are we to do? There is a watchman sitting in front of the fold." Thereon, Mr. Mighty-of-his-mouth cleared away his doubts by saying that it was no watchman, but a mere stick, and entered the fold with his friend.

It had also so happened that on that very night a *bhûta* (goblin) had come into the fold to steal away a sheep. It shuddered with fear on hearing the shepherd mention the *kûta,* for having never heard of the existence of *kûtas,* it mistook this imaginary being to be something superior in strength to itself. So thinking that a *kûta* might come to the fold, and not wishing to expose itself till it knew well what *kûtas* were, the *bhûta* transformed itself into a sheep and laid itself down among the flock. By this time the two Mighties had entered the fold and begun an examination of the sheep. They went on rejecting one animal after another for some defect or other, till at last they came to the sheep which was none other than the *bhûta*. They tested it, and when they found it very heavy—as, of course, it would be with the soul of the *bhûta* in it—they began to tie up its legs to carry it home. When hands began to shake it the *bhûta* mistook the Mighties for the *kûtas,* and said to itself:—

"Alas! the *kûtas* have come to take me away. What am I to do? What a fool I was to come into the fold!" So thought the *bhûta* as Mr. Mighty-of-his-hands was carrying it away on his head, with his friend following him behind. But the *bhûta* soon began to work its devilish powers to extricate itself, and Mr. Mighty-of-his-hands began to feel pains all over his body and said to his friend:

"My dear Mighty, I feel pains all over me. I think what we have brought is no sheep!" Mr. Mighty-of-his-mouth was inwardly alarmed at the words of his friend, but did not like to show that he was afraid. So he said:

"Then put down the sheep, and let us tear open its belly, so that we shall each have only one-half of it to carry."

This frightened the *bhûta,* and he melted away on the head of Mr. Mighty-of-his-hands, who, relieved of his devilish burden, was glad to return home safe with his friend.

The *bhûta,* too, went to its abode and there told its fellow-goblins how it had involved itself in a great trouble and how narrowly it had escaped. They all laughed at its stupidity and said, "What a great fool you are! They were not *kûtas*. In fact there are no *kûtas* in the world. They were men, and it was most stupid of you to have got yourself into their hands. Are you not ashamed to make such a fuss about your escape?" The injured *bhûta* retorted that they would not have made such remarks had they seen the *kûtas*. "Then show us these *kûtas,* as you choose to call them," said they, "and we will crush them in the twinkling of an eye." "Agreed," said the injured *bhûta,* and the next night it took them to the house of the Mighties, and said from a distance: "There is their house. I cannot approach it. Do whatever you like." The other *bhûtas* were amazed at the fear of their timid brother, and resolved among themselves to put an end to the enemies of even one member of their caste. So they went in a great crowd to the house of the Mighties. Some stood outside the house, to see that none of the inmates escaped, and some watched in the back-yard, while a score of them jumped over the walls and entered the court-yard.

Mr. Mighty-of-his-hands was sleeping in the verandah, adjoining the court-yard, and when he heard the noise of people jumping about, he opened his eyes, and to his terror saw some *bhûtas* in the court. Without opening his mouth he quietly rolled himself along the ground, and went to the room where Mr. Mighty-of-his-mouth was sleeping with his wife and children. Tapping gently at the door he awoke his friend and said:

"What shall we do now? The *bhûtas* have invaded our house, and will soon kill us."

Mr. Mighty-of-his-mouth told him quietly not to be afraid, but to go and sleep in his original place, and that he himself would make the *bhûtas* run away. Mr. Mighty-of-his-hands did not understand what his friend meant, but not wishing to argue rolled his way back to his original place and pretended to sleep, though his heart was beating terribly with fright. Mr. Mighty-of-his-mouth now awoke his wife, and instructed her thus:

"My dearest wife, the foolish *bhûtas* have invaded our house, but if you act according to my advice we are safe, and the goblins will depart harmlessly. What I want you to do is, to go to the hall and light a lamp, spread leaves on the floor, and then pretend to awake me for my supper. I shall get up and enquire what you have ready to give me to eat. You will then reply that you have only pepper water and vegetables. With an angry face I shall say, 'What have you done with the three *bhûtas* that our son caught hold of on his way back from school?' Your reply must be, 'The rogue wanted some sweetmeats on coming home. Unfortunately I had none in the house, so he roasted the three *bhûtas* and gobbled them up.'"

Thus instructing his wife Mr. Mighty-of-his-mouth pretended to go to sleep. The wife accordingly spread the leaves and called her husband for his supper. During the conversation that followed, the fact that the son had roasted three goblins for sweetmeats was conveyed to the *bhûtas*. They shuddered at the son's extraordinary ability, and thought,

"What must the father do for his meals when a son roasts three *bhûtas* for sweetmeats?"

So they at once took to their heels. Then going to the brother they had jeered at, they said to him that indeed the *kûtas* were their greatest enemies, and that none of their lives were safe while they remained where they were, as on that very evening the son of a *kûta* had roasted three of them for sweetmeats. They therefore all resolved to fly away to the adjoining forest, and disappeared accordingly. Thus Mr. Mighty-of-his-mouth saved himself and his friend on two occasions from the *bhûtas*.

The friends after this went out one day to an adjoining village and were returning home rather late in the evening. Darkness fell on them before half the way was traversed, and there lay before them a dense wood infested by beasts of prey: so they resolved to spend the night in a high tree and go home next morning, and accordingly got up into a big *pîpal*. Now this was the very wood into which the *bhûtas* had migrated, and at midnight they all came down with torches to catch jackals and other animals to feast upon. The fear of Mr. Mighty-of-his-hands may be more imagined than described. The dreaded *bhûtas* were at the foot of the very tree in which he had taken up his abode for the night! His hands trembled. His body shook. He lost his hold, and down he came with a horrible rustling of leaves. His friend, however, was, as usual, ready with a device, and bawled out:

"I wished to leave these poor beings to their own revelry. But you are hungry and must needs jump down to catch some of them. Do not fail to lay your hands on the stoutest *bhûta*."

The goblins heard the voice which was already very familiar to their ears, for was it not the *kûta* whose son had roasted up three *bhûtas* for sweetmeats that spoke? So they ran away at once, crying out:

"Alas, what misery! Our bitter enemies have followed us even to this wood!"

Thus the wit of Mr. Mighty-of-his-mouth saved himself and his friend for the third time.

The sun began to rise, and Mr. Mighty-of-his-hands thrice walked round Mr. Mighty-of-his-mouth and said:

"My dear friend, truly you only of us two are mighty. Mere physical strength is of no use without skill in words. The latter is far superior to the former, and if a man possess both, he is, as it were, a golden lotus having a sweet scent. It is enough for me now to have arrived at this moral! With your kind permission I shall return to my village." Mr. Mighty-of-his-mouth asked his friend not to consider himself under any obligation, and, after honouring him as became his position he let him return to his village.

The moral of this short story is that in man there is nothing great but mind.

# CHAPTER VIII.

## THE MOTHER-IN-LAW BECAME AN ASS.

Little by little the mother-in-law became an ass—*vara vara mâmi kaludai pôl ânâḷ*, is a proverb among the Tamiḻs, applied to those who day by day go downwards in their progress in study, position, or life, and based on the following story:—

In a certain village their lived a Brâhmaṇ with his wife, mother, and mother-in-law. He was a very good man, and equally kind to all of them. His mother complained of nothing at his hands, but his wife was a very bad-tempered woman, and always troubled her mother-in-law by keeping her engaged in this work or that throughout the day, and giving her very little food in the evening. Owing to this the poor Brâhmaṇ's mother was almost dying of misery. On the other hand, her own mother received very kind treatment, of course, at her daughter's hands, but the husband was so completely ruled by his wife, that he had no strength of mind to oppose her ill-treatment of his mother.

One evening, just before sunset, the wife abused her mother-in-law with such fury, that the latter had to fly away to escape a thrashing. Full of misery she ran out of the village, but the sun had begun to set, and the darkness of night was fast overtaking her. So finding a ruined temple she entered it to pass the night there. It happened to be the abode of the village Kâlî (goddess), who used to come out every night at midnight to inspect her village. That night she perceived a woman—the mother of the poor Brâhmaṇ—lurking within her prâkâras (boundaries), and being a most benevolent Kâlî, called out to her, and asked her what made her so miserable that she should leave her home on such a dark night. The Brâhmaṇî told her story in a few words, and while she was speaking the cunning goddess was using her supernatural powers to see whether all she said was true or not, and finding it to be the truth, she thus replied in very soothing tones:—

"I pity your misery, mother, because your daughter-in-law troubles and vexes you thus when you have become old, and have no strength in your body. Now take this mango," and taking a ripe one from out her waist-band, she gave it to the old Brâhmaṇî with a smiling face—"eat it, and you will soon become a young woman like your own daughter-in-law, and then she shall no longer trouble you." Thus consoling the afflicted old woman, the kind-hearted Kâlî went away. The Brâhmaṇî lingered for the remainder of the night in the temple, and being a fond mother she did not like to eat the whole of the mango without giving a portion of it to her son.

Meanwhile, when her son returned home in the evening he found his mother absent, but his wife explained the matter to him, so as to throw the blame on the old woman, as she always did. As it was dark he had no chance of going out to search for her, so he waited for the daylight, and as soon as he saw the dawn, started to look for his mother. He had not walked far when to his joy he found her in the temple of Kâlî.

"How did you pass the cold night, my dearest mother?" said he. "What did you have for dinner? Wretch that I am to have got myself married to a cur. Forget all her faults, and return home."

His mother shed tears of joy and sorrow, and related her previous night's adventure, upon which he said:—

"Delay not even one *nimisha* (minute), but eat this fruit at once. I do not want any of it. Only if you become young and strong enough to stand that nasty cur's troubles, well and good."

So the mother ate up the divine fruit, and the son took her upon his shoulders and brought her home, on reaching which he placed her on the ground, when to his joy she was no longer an old woman, but a young girl of sixteen, and stronger than his own wife. The troublesome wife was now totally put down, and was powerless against so strong a mother-in-law.

She did not at all like the change, and having to give up her habits of bullying, and so she argued to herself thus:—

"This jade of a mother-in-law became young through the fruit of the Kâlî, why should not my mother also do the same, if I instruct her and send her to the same temple."

So she instructed her mother as to the story she ought to give to the goddess and sent her there. Her old mother, agreeably to her daughter's injunctions, went to the temple, and on meeting with the goddess at midnight, gave a false story that she was being greatly ill-treated by her daughter-in-law, though, in truth, she had nothing of the kind to complain of. The goddess perceived the lie through her divine powers, but pretending to pity her, gave her also a fruit. Her daughter had instructed her not to eat it till next morning, and till she saw her son-in-law.

As soon as morning approached, the poor hen-pecked Brâhmaṇ was ordered by his wife to go to the temple and fetch his mother-in-law, as he had some time back fetched away his mother. He accordingly went, and invited her to come home. She wanted him to eat part of the fruit, as she had been instructed, but he refused, and so she swallowed it all, fully expecting to become young again on reaching home. Meanwhile her son-in-law took her on his shoulders and returned home, expecting, as his former experience had taught him, to see his mother-in-law also turn into a young woman. Anxiety to see how the change came on overcame him, and half way he turned his head, and found such part of the burden on his shoulders as he could see, to be like parts of an ass, but he took this to be a mere preliminary stage towards youthful womanhood! Again he turned, and again he saw the same thing several times, and the more he looked the more his burden became like an ass, till at last when he reached home, his burden jumped down braying like an ass and ran away.

Thus the Kâlî, perceiving the evil intentions of the wife, disappointed her by turning her mother into an ass, but no one knew of it till she actually jumped down from the shoulders of her son-in-law.

This story is always cited as the explanation of the proverb quoted above—*vara vara mâmi kaludai pôl ânâl*—little by little the mother-in-law became an ass, to which is also commonly added *ûr varumbôdu ûlaiyida talaippattal*—and as she approached the village, she began to bray.

# CHAPTER IX.

## THE STORY OF APPAYYA.[56]

अपूपेन हताः चोराः
हता खड्गेन केसरी ।
तुरंगेण हतं सैन्यम्
विधिर्भाग्यानु सारिणी ॥

In a remote village there lived a poor Brâhmaṇ and his wife. Though several years of their wedded life had passed, they unfortunately had no children, and so, being very eager for a child, and having no hope of one by his first wife, the poor Brâhmaṇ made up his mind to marry a second. His wife would not permit it for some time, but finding her husband resolved, she gave way, thinking within herself that she would manage somehow to do away with the second wife. As soon as he had got her consent the Brâhmaṇ arranged for his second marriage and wedded a beautiful Brâhmaṇ girl. She went to live with him in the same house with the first wife, who, thinking that she would be making the world suspicious if she did anything suddenly, waited for some time.

Iśvara himself seemed to favour the new marriage, and the second wife, a year after her wedding, becoming pregnant, went in the sixth month of her pregnancy to her mother's house for her confinement. Her husband bore his separation from her patiently for a fortnight, but after this the desire to see her again began to prey upon his mind, and he was always asking his first wife when he ought to go to her. She seemed to sympathise fully with his trouble, and said:—

"My dearest husband, your health is daily being injured, and I am glad that your love for her has not made it worse than it is. To-morrow you must start on a visit to her. It is said that we should not go empty-handed to children, a king, or a pregnant woman; so I shall give you one hundred *apûpa* cakes, packed up separately in a vessel, which you must give to her. You are very fond of *apûpas* and I fear that you will eat some of them on the way; but you had better not do so. And I will give you some cakes packed in a cloth separately for you to eat on your journey."

So the first wife spent the whole night in preparing the *apûpa* cakes, and mixed poison in the sugar and rice-flour of those she made for her co-wife and rival; but as she entertained no enmity against her husband the *apûpas* cakes for him were

[56] [Compare the tale of Fattû, the Valiant Weaver, *Indian Antiquary*, Vol. XI., p. 282 ff.—R. C. T.]

properly prepared. By the time the morning dawned she had packed up the hundred *apûpas* in a brass vessel which could be easily carried on a man's head.

After a light breakfast—for a heavy one is always bad before a journey on foot—the Brâhmaṇ placed the brass vessel on his head, and holding in his hand the kerchief containing the food for himself on the way, started for the village of his second wife, which happened to be at a distance of two days' journey. He walked in hot haste till evening approached, and when the darkness of night overtook him the rapidity of his walk had exhausted him, and he felt very hungry. He espied a wayside shed and a tank near his path, and entered the water to perform his evening ablution to the god of the day, who was fast going down below the horizon. As soon as this was over he untied his kerchief, and did full justice to its contents by swallowing every cake whole. He then drank some water, and being quite overcome by fatigue, fell into a deep slumber in the shed, with his brass vessel and its sweet, or rather poisonous, contents under his head.

Close by the spot where the Brâhmaṇ slept there reigned a famous king who had a very beautiful daughter. Several persons demanded her hand in marriage, among whom was a robber chieftain who wanted her for his only son. Though the king liked the boy for his beauty, the thought that he was only a robber for all that prevented him from making up his mind to give his daughter in marriage to him. The robber chief, however, was determined to have his own way, and accordingly despatched one hundred of his band to fetch away the princess in the night without her knowledge while she was sleeping, to his palace in the woods. In obedience to their chieftain's order the robbers, on the night the Brâhmaṇ happened to sleep in the shed, entered the king's palace and stole away the princess, together with the bed on which she was sleeping. On reaching the shed the hundred robbers found themselves very thirsty—for being awake at midnight always brings on thirst. So they placed the cot on the ground and were entering the water to quench their thirst; just then they smelt the *apûpa* cakes, which, for all that they contained poison, had a very sweet savour. The robbers searched about the shed, and found the Brâhmaṇ sleeping on one side and the brass vessel lying at a distance from him, for he had pushed it from underneath his head when he had stretched himself in his sleep; they opened the vessel, and to their joy found in it exactly one hundred *apûpa* cakes.

"We have one here for each of us, and that is something better than mere water. Let us each eat before we go into it," said the leader of the gang, and at once each man swallowed greedily what he had in his hand, and immediately all fell down dead. Lucky it was that no one knew of the old Brâhmaṇî's trick. Had the robbers had any reason to suspect it they would never have eaten the cakes; had the Brâhmaṇ known it he would never have brought them with him for his dear second wife. Lucky was it for the poor old Brâhmaṇ and his second wife, and lucky was it for the sleeping princess, that these cakes went, after all, into the stomachs of the villainous robbers!

After sleeping his fill the Brâhmaṇ, who had been dreaming of his second wife all night, awoke in haste to pursue the remainder of his journey to her house. He could not find his brass vessel, but near the place where he had left it he found several men of the woods, whom he knew very well by their appearance to be robbers, as he thought, sleeping. Angered at the loss of his vessel he took up a sword from one of the dead robbers and cut off all their heads, thinking all the while that he was killing one hundred living robbers, who were sleeping after having eaten all his cakes. Presently the princess's cot fell under his gaze, and he approached it and found on it a most beautiful lady fast asleep. Being an intelligent man he perceived that the persons whose heads he had cut off must have been some thieves, or other wicked men, who had carried her off. He was not long in doubt, for not far off he saw an army marching up rapidly with a king at its head, who was saying, "Down with the robber who has stolen away my daughter." The Brâhmaṇ at once inferred that this must be the father of the sleeping princess, and suddenly waking her up from her sleep spoke thus to her:—

"Behold before you the hundred robbers that brought you here a few hours ago from your palace. I fought one and all of them single-handed, and have killed them all."

The princess was highly pleased at what she heard, for she knew of all the tricks the robbers had previously played to carry her off. So she fell reverently at the Brâhmaṇ's feet and said:—

"Friend, never till now have I heard of a warrior who, single-handed, fought one hundred robbers. Your valour is unparalleled. I *will* be your wife, if only in remembrance of your having saved me from falling into the hands of these ruffians."

Her father and his army was now near the shed, for he had all along watched the conduct of the robber chieftain, and as soon as the maid-servants of the palace informed him of the disappearance of the princess and her bed, he marched straight with his soldiers for the woods. His joy, when he saw his daughter safe, knew no bounds, and he flew into his daughter's arms, while she pointed to the Brâhmaṇ as her preserver. The king now put a thousand questions to our hero, who, being well versed in matters of fighting, gave sound replies, and so came successfully out of his first adventure. The king, astonished at his valour, took him to his palace, and rewarded him with the hand of the princess. And the robber chieftain, fearing the new son-in-law, who, single-handed, had killed a hundred of his robbers, never troubled himself about the princess. Thus the Brâhmaṇ's first adventure ended in making him son-in-law to a king!

Now there lived a lioness in a wood near the princess's country, who had a great taste for human flesh, and so, once a week, the king used to send a man into the wood to serve as her prey. All the people now collected together before the king, and said:—

"Most honoured king, while you have a son-in-law who killed one hundred robbers with his sword, why should you continue to send a man into the wood every week. We request you to send your son-in-law next week to the wood and have the lioness killed."

This seemed most reasonable to the king, who called for his son-in-law, and sent him, armed to the teeth, into the wood.

Now our Brâhmaṇ could not refuse to go, for fear of losing the fame of his former exploit, and, hoping that fortune would favour him, he asked his father-in-law to have him hoisted up into a big banyan tree with all kinds of weapons, and this was done. The appointed time for the lioness to eat her prey approached, and as she saw no one coming for her, and as sometimes those that had to come used to linger for a short time in the tree in which the Brâhmaṇ had taken refuge, she went up to it to see that no such trick has been played upon her this time. This made the Brâhmaṇ tremble so violently that he dropped the sword he held in his hand. At that very moment the lioness happened to yawn, and the sword dropped right into her jaws and killed her. As soon as the Brâhmaṇ saw the course which events had taken, he came down from the tree, and invented a thousand stories of how he had given battle to the terrible lioness and overcome her. This exploit fully established his valour, and feasts and rejoicings in honour of it followed, and the whole country round blessed the son-in-law of their king.

Near this kingdom there also reigned a powerful emperor, who levied tribute from all the surrounding countries. To this emperor the father-in-law of our most valorous Brâhmaṇ, who, at one stroke, had killed one hundred robbers, and, at another, a fierce lioness, had also to pay a certain amount of tribute; but, trusting to the power of his son-in-law, he stopped the tribute to the emperor, who, by the way, was named Appayya Râja, and who, as soon as the tribute was stopped, invaded his dominions, and his father-in-law besought the Brâhmaṇ for assistance.

Again the poor Brâhmaṇ could not refuse, for, if he did, all his former fame would have been lost; so he determined to undertake this adventure also, and to trust to fortune rather than give up the attempt. He asked for the best horse and the sharpest sword, and set out to fight the enemy, who had already encamped on the other side of the river, which flowed at a short distance to the east of the town.

Now the king had a very unruly horse, which had never been broken in, and this he gave his son-in-law; and, supplying him with a sharp sword, asked him to start. The Brâhmaṇ then asked the king's servants to tie him up with cotton strings tight on to the saddle, and set out on the expedition.

The horse, having never till then felt a man on its back, began to gallop most furiously, and flew onwards so fast that all who saw it thought the rider must lose his life, and he too was almost dead with fear. He tried his best to curb his steed, but the more he pulled the faster it galloped, till giving up all hopes of life he let it take its course. It jumped into the water and swam across to the other side of the river, wetting the cotton cords by which the Brâhmaṇ was tied down to the saddle, making them swell and giving him the most excruciating pain. He bore it, however, with all the patience imaginable. Presently the horse reached the other side of the river, where there was a big palmyra tree, which a recent flood had left almost uprooted and ready to fall at the slightest touch. The Brâhmaṇ, unable to stop the course of the horse, held fast on to the tree, hoping thus to check its wild career. But unfortunately for him the tree gave way, and the steed galloped on so furiously that he did not know which was the safer—to leave the tree or to hold on to it. Meanwhile the wet cotton cords hurt him so that he, in the hopelessness of despair, bawled out *appa! ayya!*[57] On went his steed, and still he held on to the palmyra tree. Though now fighting for his own life, the people that were watching him from a great distance thought him to be flying to the battlefield, armed with a palmyra tree! The cry of lamentation, *appa ayya,* which he uttered, his enemy mistook for a challenge, because, as we know, his name happened to be Appayya. Horror-struck at the sight of a warrior armed with a huge tree, his enemy turned and fled. *Yathâ râjâ tathâ prajâh*—"As is the king so are the subjects,"—and accordingly his followers also fled. The Brâhmaṇ warrior (!) seeing the fortunate course events had again taken pursued the enemy, or rather let his courser have its own furious way. Thus the enemy and his vast army melted away in the twinkling of an eye, and the horse, too, when it became exhausted, returned towards the palace.

The old king had been watching from the loftiest rooms of his palace all that had passed on the other side of the river, and believing his son-in-law had, by his own prowess, driven out the enemy, approached him with all pomp. Eager hands quickly cut the knots by which the victorious (!) Brâhmaṇ had been held tight in his saddle, and his old father-in-law with tears of joy embraced him on his victory, saying that the whole kingdom was indebted to him. A splendid triumphal march was conducted, in which the eyes of the whole town were directed towards our victorious hero.

Thus, on three different occasions, and in three different adventures, fortune favoured the poor Brâhmaṇ and brought him fame. He then sent for his two former wives and took them into his palace. His second wife, who was pregnant when he first started with the *apûpa* cakes to see her, had given birth to a male child, who was, when she came back to him, more than a year old. The first wife confessed to her husband her sin of having given him poisoned cakes, and craved his pardon; and it was only now that he came to know that the hundred robbers he killed in his first adventure were all really dead men, and that they must have died from the effects of the poison in the cakes, and, since her treachery had given him a new start in life, he forgave her. She, too, gave up her enmity to the partners of her husband's bed, and all the four lived in peace and plenty for many a long day afterwards.

[57] Which in Tamil are exclamations of lamentation, meaning, Ah! Alas!

# CHAPTER X.

## THE BRÂHMIṆ GIRL THAT MARRIED A TIGER.

In a certain village there lived an old Brâhmiṇ who had three sons and a daughter. The girl being the youngest was brought up most tenderly and became spoilt, and so whenever she saw a beautiful boy she would say to her parents that she must be wedded to him. Her parents were, therefore, much put about to devise excuses for taking her away from her youthful lovers. Thus passed on some years, till the girl was very nearly grown up, and then the parents, fearing that they would be driven out of their caste if they failed to dispose of her hand in marriage before she came to the years of maturity, began to be eager about finding a bridegroom for her.

Now near their village there lived a fierce tiger, that had attained to great proficiency in the art of magic, and had the power of assuming different forms. Having a great taste for Brâhmiṇ's food, the tiger used now and then to frequent temples and other places of public refreshment in the shape of an old famished Brâhmiṇ in order to share the food prepared for the Brâhmiṇs. The tiger also wanted, if possible, a Brâhmiṇ wife to take to the woods, and there to make her cook his meals after her fashion. One day, when he was partaking of his meals in Brâhmiṇ shape at a *satra*[58], he heard the talk about the Brâhmiṇ girl who was always falling in love with every beautiful Brâhmiṇ boy.

Said he to himself, "Praised be the face that I saw first this morning. I shall assume the shape of a Brâhmiṇ boy, and appear as beautiful can be, and win the heart of the girl."

Next morning he accordingly became in the form of a great Śâstrin (proficient in the *Râmâyaṇa*) and took his seat near the *ghâṭ* of the sacred river of the village. Scattering holy ashes profusely over his body he opened the *Râmâyaṇa* and began to read.

"The voice of the new Śâstrin is most enchanting. Let us go and hear him," said some women among themselves, and sat down before him to hear him expound the great book. The girl for whom the tiger had assumed this shape came in due time to bathe at the river, and as soon as she saw the new Śâstrin fell in love with him, and bothered her old mother to speak to her father about him, so as not to lose her new lover. The old woman too was delighted at the bridegroom whom fortune had thrown in her way, and ran home to her husband, who, when he came and saw the Śâstrin, raised up his hands in praise of the great god Mahêśvara. The

[58] A place of public feeding.

Śâstrin was now invited to take his meals with them, and as he had come with the express intention of marrying the daughter, he, of course, agreed.

A grand dinner followed in honour of the Śâstrin, and his host began to question him as to his parentage, &c., to which the cunning tiger replied that he was born in a village beyond the adjacent wood. The Brâhmiṇ had no time to wait for further enquiries, and as the boy was very fair he married his daughter to him the very next day. Feasts followed for a month, during which time the bridegroom gave every satisfaction to his new relatives, who supposed him to be human all the while. He also did full justice to the Brâhmiṇ dishes, and swallowed everything that was placed before him.

After the first month was over the tiger-bridegroom bethought him of his accustomed prey, and hankered after his abode in the woods. A change of diet for a day or two is all very well, but to renounce his own proper food for more than a month was hard. So one day he said to his father-in-law, "I must go back soon to my old parents, for they will be pining at my absence. But why should we have to bear the double expense of my coming all the way here again to take my wife to my village? So if you will kindly let me take the girl with me I shall take her to her future home, and hand her over to her mother-in-law, and see that she is well taken care of."

The old Brâhmiṇ agreed to this, and replied, "My dear son-in-law, you are her husband, and she is yours, and we now send her with you, though it is like sending her into the wilderness with her eyes tied up. But as we take you to be everything to her, we trust you to treat her kindly."

The mother of the bride shed tears at the idea of having to send her away, but nevertheless the very next day was fixed for the journey. The old woman spent the whole day in preparing cakes and sweetmeats for her daughter, and when the time for the journey arrived, she took care to place in her bundles and on her head one or two margosa[59] leaves to keep off demons. The relatives of the bride requested her husband to allow her to rest wherever she found shade, and to eat wherever she found water, and to this he agreed, and so they began their journey.

The boy tiger and his human wife pursued their journey for two or three *ghaṭikâs*[60] in free and pleasant conversation, when the girl happened to see a fine pond, round which the birds were warbling their sweet notes. She requested her husband to follow her to the water's edge and to partake of some of the cakes and sweetmeats with her.

But he replied, "Be quiet, or I shall show you my original shape."

This made her afraid, so she pursued her journey in silence until she saw another pond, when she asked the same question of her husband, who replied in the same tone.

[59] Among high caste Hindûs, when girls leave one village and go to another, the old woman of the house—the mother or grandmother—always places in her bundles and on her head a few margosa leaves as a talisman against demons.

[60] A *ghaṭikâ* is twenty-four minutes. The story being Hindu, the Hindû method of reckoning distance is used.

Now she was very hungry, and not liking her husband's tone, which she found had greatly changed ever since they had entered the woods, said to him,

"Show me your original shape."

No sooner were these words uttered than her husband's form changed from that of a man. Four legs, striped skin, a long tail, and a tiger's face came over him suddenly and, horror of horrors! a tiger and not a man stood before her! Nor were her fears stilled when the tiger in human voice began as follows:—

"Know henceforth that I, your husband, am a tiger—this very tiger that now speaks to you. If you have any regard for your life you must obey all my orders implicitly, for I can speak to you in human voice, and understand what you say. In a couple of *ghaṭikâs* we shall reach my home, of which you will become the mistress. In the front of my house you will see half-a-dozen tubs, each of which you must fill up daily with some dish or other, cooked in your own way. I shall take care to supply you with all the provisions you want." So saying the tiger slowly conducted her to his house.

The misery of the girl may more be imagined than described, for if she were to object she would be put to death. So, weeping all the way, she reached her husband's house. Leaving her there he went out and returned with several pumpkins and some flesh, of which she soon prepared a curry and gave it to her husband. He went out again after this and returned in the evening with several vegetables and some more flesh, and gave her an order:—

"Every morning I shall go out in search of provisions and prey, and bring something with me on my return; you must keep cooked for me whatever I leave in the house."

So next morning as soon as the tiger had gone away she cooked everything left in the house and filled all the tubs with food. At the tenth *ghaṭikâ* the tiger returned and growled out,

"I smell a man! I smell a woman in my wood." And his wife for very fear shut herself up in the house.

As soon as the tiger had satisfied his appetite he told her to open the door, which she did, and they talked together for a time, after which the tiger rested awhile, and then went out hunting again. Thus passed many a day, till the tiger's Brâhmiṇ wife had a son, which also turned out to be only a tiger.

One day, after the tiger had gone out to the woods, his wife was crying all alone in the house, when a crow happened to peck at some rice that was scattered near her, and seeing the girl crying, began to shed tears.

"Can you assist me?" asked the girl.

"Yes," said the crow.

So she brought out a palmyra leaf and wrote on it with an iron nail all her sufferings in the wood, and requested her brothers to come and relieve her. This palmyra leaf she tied to the neck of the crow, which, seeming to understand her thoughts, flew to her village and sat down before one of her brothers. He untied the leaf and read the contents of the letter and told them to his other brothers. All the three then started for the wood, asking their mother to give them something to eat on the way. She had not enough rice for the three, so she made a big ball of clay and stuck it over with what rice she had, so as to make it look like a ball of rice. This she gave to the brothers to eat on their way, and started them off to the woods.

They had not proceeded long before they espied an ass. The youngest, who was of a playful disposition, wished to take the ass with him. The two elder brothers objected to this for a time, but in the end they allowed him to have his own way. Further on they saw an ant, which the middle brother took with him. Near the ant there was a big palmyra tree lying on the ground, which the eldest took with him to keep off the tiger.

The sun was now high in the horizon and the three brothers became very hungry. So they sat down near a tank and opened the bundle containing the ball of rice. To their utter disappointment they found it to be all clay, but being extremely hungry they drank all the water in the pond and continued their journey. On leaving the tank they found a big iron tub belonging to the washerman of the adjacent village. This they took also with them in addition to the ass, the ant, and the palmyra tree. Following the road described by their sister in her letter sent by the crow, they walked on and on till they reached the tiger's house.

The sister, overjoyed to see her brothers again, ran out at once to welcome them.

"My dearest brothers, I am so glad to see that you have come here to relieve me after all, but the time for the tiger's coming home is approaching, so hide yourselves in the loft, and wait till he is gone."

So saying, she helped her brothers to ascend into the loft. By this time the tiger returned, and perceived the presence of human beings by the peculiar smell. He asked his wife whether any one had come to their house. She said, "No." But when the brothers, who with their trophies of the way—the ass, the ant, and so on—were sitting upon the loft, saw the tiger dallying with their sister, they were greatly frightened; so much so that the youngest, through fear, began to quake, and they all fell on the floor.

"What is all this?" said the terrified tiger to his wife.

"Nothing," said she, "but your brothers-in-law. They came here a watch[61] ago, and as soon as you have finished your meals they want to see you."

"How can my brothers-in-law be such cowards," thought the tiger to himself.

He then asked them to speak to him, whereon the youngest brother put the ant which he had in his hand into the ear of the ass, and as soon as the latter was bitten, it began to bawl out most horribly.

"How is it that your brothers have such a hoarse voice?" said the tiger to his wife.

[61] A "watch" is a *yâma,* or three hours.

He next asked them to show him their legs. Taking courage at the stupidity of the tiger on the two former occasions, the eldest brother now stretched out the palmyra tree.

"By my father, I have never seen such a leg," said the tiger, and asked his brothers-in-law to show their bellies. The second brother now showed the tub, at which the tiger shuddered, and saying, "such a harsh voice, so stout a leg, and such a belly, truly I have never heard of such persons as these!" He ran away.

It was already dark, and the brothers, wishing to take advantage of the tiger's terror, prepared to return home with their sister at once. They ate up what little food she had, and ordered her to start. Fortunately for her her tiger-child was asleep. So she tore it into two pieces and suspended them over the hearth, and, thus getting rid of the child, she ran off with her brothers towards home.

Before leaving she bolted the front door from inside, and went out at the back of the house. As soon as the pieces of the cub, which were hung up over the hearth, began to roast, they dripped, which made the fire hiss and sputter; and when the tiger returned at about midnight, he found the door shut and heard the hissing of the fire, which he mistook for the noise of cooking muffins.[62]

"I see," said he to himself, "how very cunning you are; you have bolted the door and are cooking muffins for your brothers. Let us see if we can't get your muffins."

So saying he went round to the back door and entered his house, and was greatly perplexed to find his cub torn in two and being roasted, his house deserted by his Brâhmiṇ wife, and his property plundered; for his wife, before leaving, had taken with her as much of the tiger's property as she could conveniently carry.

The tiger now discovered all the treachery of his wife, and his heart grieved for the loss of his son, that was now no more. He determined to be revenged on his wife, and to bring her back into the wood, and there tear her into many pieces in place of only two. But how to bring her back? He assumed his original shape of a young bridegroom, making, of course, due allowance for the number of years that had passed since his marriage, and next morning went to his father-in-law's house. His brothers-in-law and his wife saw from a distance the deceitful form he had assumed, and devised means to kill him. Meanwhile the tiger Brâhmiṇ approached his father-in-law's house, and the old people welcomed him. The younger ones too ran here and there to bring provisions to feed him sumptuously, and the tiger was highly pleased at the hospitable way in which he was received.

There was a ruined well at the back of the house, and the eldest of the brothers placed some thin sticks across its mouth, over which he spread a fine mat. Now it is usual to ask guests to have an oil bath before dinner, and so his three brothers-in-law requested the tiger to take his seat on the fine mat for his bath. As soon as he sat on it, the thin sticks being unable to bear his weight, gave way, and down fell the cunning tiger with a heavy crash! The well was at once filled in with stones and other rubbish, and thus the tiger was effectually prevented from doing any more mischief.

[62] Tamiḻ, *tô'sai.*

But the Brâhmiṇ girl, in memory of her having married a tiger, raised a pillar over the well and planted a *tulaśi*[63] shrub on the top of it. Morning and evening, for the rest of her life, she used to smear the pillar with sacred cowdung, and water the *tulaśi* shrub.

This story is told to explain the Tamil proverb, "*Śummâ irukkiraya, śuruvattai kâṭṭaṭṭuma,*" which means—

"Be quiet, or I shall show you my original shape."

---

[63] A fragrant herb, held in great veneration by the Hindûs; *Ocymum sanctum*. This herb is sacred alike to Śiva and Vishnu. Those species specially sacred to Śiva are—*Vendulasî, Śiru-tulasî,* and *Śiva-tulasî*; those to Vishnu are *Śendulasî, Karundulasî* and *Vishnu-tulasî.*

# CHAPTER XI.

## THE GOOD HUSBAND AND THE BAD WIFE.

In a remote village there lived a Brâhmiṇ whose good nature and charitable disposition were proverbial. Equally proverbial also were the ill-nature and uncharitable disposition of the Brâhmaṇî—his wife. But as Paramêśvara (God) had joined them in matrimony, they had to live together as husband and wife, though their temperaments were so incompatible. Every day the Brâhmiṇ had a taste of his wife's ill-temper, and if any other Brâhmiṇ was invited to dinner by him, his wife, somehow or other, would manage to drive him away.

One fine summer morning a rather stupid Brâhmiṇ friend of his came to visit our hero and was at once invited to dinner. He told his wife to have dinner ready earlier than usual, and went off to the river to bathe. His friend not feeling very well that day wanted a hot bath at the house, and so did not follow him to the river, but remained sitting in the outer verandah. If any other guest had come, the wife would have accused him of greediness to his face and sent him away, but this visitor seemed to be a special friend of her lord, so she did not like to say anything; but she devised a plan to make him go away of his own accord.

She proceeded to smear the ground before her husband's friend with cowdung, and placed in the midst of it a long pestle, supporting one end of it against the wall. She next approached the pestle most solemnly and performed worship (*pûjâ*) to it. The guest did not in the least understand what she was doing, and respectfully asked her what it all meant.

"This is what is called pestle worship," she replied. "I do it as a daily duty, and this pestle is intended to break the head of some human being in honour of a goddess, whose feet are most devoutly worshipped by my husband. Every day as soon as he returns from his bath in the river, he takes this pestle, which I am ordered to keep ready for him before his return, and with it breaks the head of any human being whom he has managed to get hold of by inviting him to a meal. This is his tribute (*dakshiṇâ*) to the goddess; to-day you are the victim."

The guest was much alarmed.

"What! break the head of a guest! I at any rate shall not be deceived to-day," thought he, and prepared to run away.

The Brâhmiṇ's wife appeared to sympathise with his sad plight, and said:—

"Really, I do pity you. But there is one thing you can do now to save yourself. If you go out by the front door and walk down the street my husband may follow you, so you had better go out by the back door."

To this plan the guest most thankfully agreed, and hastily ran off by the back door.

Almost immediately our hero returned from his bath, but before he could arrive his wife had cleaned up the place she had prepared for the pestle worship, and when the Brâhmiṇ, not finding his friend in the house inquired of her as to what had become of him, she said in seeming anger:—

"The greedy brute! he wanted me to give him this pestle—this very pestle which I brought forty years ago as a dowry from my mother's house, and when I refused he ran away by the back-yard in haste."

But her kind-hearted lord observed that he would rather lose the pestle than his guest, even though it was a part of his wife's dowry, and more than forty years old. So he ran off with the pestle in his hand after his friend, crying out,

"Oh Brâhmiṇ! Oh Brâhmiṇ! Stop please, and take the pestle."

But the story told by the old woman now seemed all the more true to the guest when he saw her husband running after him, and so he said,

"You and your pestle may go where you please. Never more will you catch me in your house," and ran away.

# CHAPTER XII.

## THE GOOD WIFE AND THE BAD HUSBAND.[64]

In a remote village there lived a man and his wife, who was a stupid little woman and believed everything that was told her. Whenever people wanted anything from her they used to come and flatter her; but this had to be done in the absence of her husband, because he was a very miserly man, and would never part with any of his money, for all he was exceedingly rich. Nevertheless, without his knowledge cunning beggars would now and then come to his wife and beg of her, and they used generally to succeed, as she was so amenable to flattery. But whenever her husband found her out he would come down heavily upon her, sometimes with words and sometimes with blows. Thus quarrels arose, till at last, for the sake of peace, the wife had to give up her charitable propensities.

Now there lived in the village a rogue of the first water, who had many a time witnessed what took place in the rich miser's family. Wishing to revive his old habit of getting what he wanted from the miser's wife he watched his opportunity and one day, when the miser had gone out on horseback to inspect his land, he came to his wife in the middle of the day and fell down at the threshold as if overcome by exhaustion. She ran up to him at once and asked him who he was.

"I am a native of Kailâsa," said he, "sent down by an old couple living there, for news of their son and his wife."

"Who are those fortunate dwellers on Śiva's mountain?" said she.

On this the rogue gave the names of her husband's deceased parents, which he had taken good care, of course, to learn from the neighbours.

"Do you really come from them?" said she. "Are they doing well there? Dear old people. How glad my husband would be to see you, were he here! Sit down please, and take rest awhile till he returns. How do they live there? Have they enough to eat and to dress themselves?"

These and a thousand other questions she put to the rogue, who, for his part, wanted to get away as quick as possible, as he knew full well how he would be treated if the miser should return while he was there, so he said:—

"Mother, language has no words to describe the miseries they are undergoing in the other world. They have not a rag to cover themselves, and for the last six days they have eaten nothing, and have lived on water only. It would break your heart to see them."

---

[64] Compare the Singalese folktale given on p. 62, Vol I. of the *Orientalist*.—Ed.

The rogue's pathetic words fully deceived the good woman, who firmly believed that he had come down from Kailâsa, sent by the old couple to her.

"Why should they suffer so?" said she, "when their son has plenty to eat and to dress himself, and when their daughter-in-law wears all sorts of costly ornaments?"

With that she went into the house and came out with two boxes containing all the clothes of herself and her husband, and gave the whole lot to the rogue, with instructions to take them to her poor old people in Kailâsa. She also gave him her jewel box for her mother-in-law.

"But dress and jewels will not fill their hungry stomachs," said he.

Requesting him to wait a little, the silly woman brought out her husband's cash chest and emptied the contents into the rogue's coat,[65] who now went off in haste, promising to give everything to the good people in Kailâsa. Our good lady in accordance with etiquette, conducted him a few hundred yards along the road and sent news of herself through him to her relatives, and then returned home. The rogue now tied up all his booty in his coat and ran in haste towards the river and crossed over it.

No sooner had our heroine reached home than her husband returned after his inspection of his lands. Her pleasure at what she had done was so great, that she met him at the door and told him all about the arrival of the messenger from Kailâsa, and how she had sent clothes, and jewels, and money through him to her husband's parents. The anger of her husband knew no bounds. But he checked himself for a while, and asked her which road the messenger from Kailâsa had taken, as he said he wanted to follow him and send some more news to his parents. To this she willingly agreed and pointed out the direction the rogue had gone. With rage in his heart at the trick played upon his stupid wife, our hero rode on in hot haste, and after a ride of two *ghaṭikâs* he caught sight of the departing rogue, who, finding escape hopeless, climbed up into a big *pîpal* tree. Our hero soon reached the bottom of the tree and shouted to the rogue to come down.

"No, I cannot, this is the way to Kailâsa," said the rogue, and climbed up on the top of the tree.

Seeing no chance of the rogue's coming down, and as there was no third person present to whom he could call for help, our hero tied his horse to an adjacent tree and began climbing up the *pîpal* tree himself. The rogue thanked all his gods when he saw this, and waited till his enemy had climbed nearly up to him, and then, throwing down his bundle of booty, leapt quickly from branch to branch till he reached the bottom. He then got upon his enemy's horse, and with his bundle rode into a dense forest in which no one was likely to find him.

Our hero being much older in years was no match for the rogue. So he slowly came down, and cursing his stupidity in having risked his horse to recover his property, returned home at his leisure. His wife, who was waiting his arrival, welcomed him with a cheerful countenance and said:—

[65] *Uparani* or *upavastra,* an upper garment.

"I thought as much, you have sent away your horse to Kailâsa to be used by your father."

Vexed as he was at his wife's words, our hero replied in the affirmative to conceal his own stupidity.

Thus, some there are in this world, who, though they may not willingly give away anything, pretend to have done so when, by accident, or stupidity, they happen to lose it.

# CHAPTER XIII.

## THE LOST CAMEL AND OTHER TALES.

### FIRST PART.

There was a city called Alakapuri, famous for all the riches that sea and land can yield, and inhabited by people speaking different languages. In that city reigned a king named Alakesa, who was a storehouse of all excellent qualities. He was so just a king that during his reign the cow and the tiger amicably quenched their thirst side by side in the same pond, the cats and the rats sported in one and the same spot, and the kite and the parrot laid their eggs in the same nest, as though they were "birds of a feather."[66] The women never deviated from the path of virtue, and regarded their husbands as gods. Timely rain refreshed the soil, and all Alakesa's subjects lived in plenty and happiness. In short, Alakesa was the body, and his subjects the soul of that body, for he was upright in all things.

Now there was in Alakapuri a rich merchant who lost a camel one day. He searched for it without success in all directions, and at last reached a road which he was informed led to another city, called Mathurapuri, the king of which was named Mathuresa. He had under him four excellent ministers, whose names were Bodhaditya, Bodhachandra, Bodhavyapaka, and Bodhavibhishana. These four ministers, being, for some reason, displeased with the king, quitted his dominions, and set out for another country. As they journeyed along they observed the track of a camel, and each made a remark on the peculiar condition of the animal, judging from the footsteps and other indications on the road.[67]

Presently they met the merchant who was searching for his camel, and, entering into conversation with him, one of the travellers inquired if the animal was not lame in one of its legs; another asked if it was not blind of the right eye; the

---

[66] This kind of statement often occurs in stories in proof of the just reign of a monarch. The Hindu idea is that so long as justice and equity characterise a king's rule, even beasts naturally inimical are disposed to live in friendship. When timely rain fails or famine stalks through the land, turning his eyes from the natural causes, the orthodox Hindu will say that such a king is now reigning over them unjustly, and hence the calamity.—*Translator.*

[67] "Distinguishing the peculiarities of an animal by its footsteps, &c., is often met with in Indian stories. Precisely the reverse of this is the tale of the four *blind* men who disputed about the form of an elephant. One of them had felt only the elephant's ears, and said it was like a winnow; another examined the breast and a foreleg, and said it was like a thick stump of wood; the third felt the trunk, and said it was like a heavy crook; while the fourth, having touched only the tail, declared it was like a sweeping rake."—*W. A. Clouston.*

third asked if its tail was not unusually short; and the fourth inquired if it was not suffering from colic. They were all answered in the affirmative by the merchant, who was convinced that they must have seen the animal, and eagerly demanded where they had seen it. They replied that they had seen traces of the camel, but not the camel itself, which being inconsistent with the minute description they had given of it, the merchant accused them of having stolen the beast, and immediately applied to king Alakesa for redress.

On hearing the merchant's story, the king was equally impressed with the belief that the travellers must know what had become of the camel, and sending for them threatened them with his displeasure if they did not confess the truth. How could they know, he demanded, that the camel was lame or blind, or whether the tail was long or short, or that it was suffering from any malady, unless they had it in their possession? In reply, they each explained the reasons which had induced them to express their belief in these particulars. The first traveller said:—

"I noticed in the footmarks of the animal that one was deficient, and I concluded accordingly that it was lame of one of its legs."

The second said:—"I noticed that the leaves of the trees on the left side of the road had been snapped or torn off, whilst those on the right side were untouched, whence I concluded that the animal was blind of his right eye."

The third said:—"I saw some drops of blood on the road, which I conjectured had flowed from the bites of gnats or flies, and I thence concluded that the camel's tail was shorter than usual, in consequence of which he could not brush the insects away."

The fourth said:—"I observed that while the forefeet of the animal were planted firmly on the ground the hind ones appeared to have scarcely touched it, whence I guessed that they were contracted by pain in the belly of the animal."

When the king heard their explanation he was much struck by the sagacity of the travellers, and giving 500 pagodas to the merchant who had lost the camel; he made the four young men his principal ministers, and bestowed on each of them several villages as free gifts.

# THE THREE CALAMITIES.

From that time these four young men became the confidential advisers of king Alakesa in all important affairs of state, and, as night is the house of sins, they in turn kept a regular watch in the city of Alakapuri, each patrolling the streets during three hours of the night. Thus they continued to faithfully serve king Alakesa, till one night, the First Minister, when his watch was over, proceeded as usual, to see whether the royal bedchamber was properly guarded; after which he went to the temple of the goddess Kâlî, where he heard what seemed to him the voice of a woman, lamenting and sobbing in great distress. Concealing himself behind the *vad*-tree of the temple, he called out:—

"Who are you, poor woman? and why do you thus weep?"

At once the cries ceased, and a voice from the temple inquired:—

"Who art thou that thus questionest me?"

Then the minister knew that it was Kâlî herself who wept; so he threw himself on the ground, and, rising up, exclaimed:—

"O, my mother!—Kâlî!—Sambhavi!—Mahamayi![68] Why should you thus weep?" quoth Kâlî.

"What is the use of my revealing it to thee? Canst thou render any assistance?"

The minister said that, if he had but her favour, there was nothing he could not do. Then the goddess told him that a calamity was about to come upon the king, and fearing that such a good monarch was soon to disappear from the world, she wept.

The thought of such a misfortune caused the minister to tremble; he fell down before the goddess, and with tears streaming from his eyes besought her to save him. Kâlî was much gratified to observe his devotion to his master, and thus addressed him:—

"Know, then, that your king will be in danger of three calamities to-morrow, any one of which will be sufficient to cause his death. First of all, early in the morning, there will come to the palace several carts containing newly-reaped paddy grains. The king will be delighted at this, and immediately order a measure of the paddy to be shelled and cooked for his morning meal. Now, the field in which that paddy grew is the abode of serpents, two of which were fighting together one

[68] The night-watch hearing the tutelary goddess of the village mourning, is a very ancient idea. It also occurs, for example, in the story of Viravara, in the Sanskrit book of fables entitled "Hitopadesa." Sambhavi and Mahamayi are different names of Kâlî—a fierce goddess, much worshipped as the presiding deity of cholera and smallpox.—*T.*

day, when they emitted poison, which has permeated those grains. Therefore, the morning meal of your king will contain poison, but only in the first handful will it take effect and he will die. Should he escape, another calamity is in store for him at noon. The king of Vijayanagara will send to-morrow some baskets of sweetmeats; in the first basket he has concealed arrows. King Alakesa, suspecting no treachery, will order the first basket to be opened in his presence, and will meet his death by that device. And even should he escape this second calamity, a third will put an end to his life to-morrow night. A deadly serpent will descend into his bed room, by means of the chain of his hanging bed, and bite him. But, should he be saved from this last misfortune, Alakesa will live long and prosperously, till he attains the age of a hundred and twenty years."

Thus spake Kâlî, in tones of sorrow, for she feared that the king would lose his life by one of these three calamities. The Minister prostrated himself on the ground, and said that if the goddess would grant him her favour he was confident he could contrive to avert all the threatened evils from the king. Kâlî smiled and disappeared; and the Minister, taking her kind smile as a token of her favour, returned home and slept soundly.

As soon as morning dawned, the First Minister arose, and having made the customary ablutions, proceeded to the palace. He took care to reveal to no one the important secret communicated to him by the goddess—not even to his three colleagues. The sun was not yet two *ghaṭikâs*[69] above the horizon when several carts containing the finest paddy grains, specially selected for the king's use, came into the courtyard of the palace. Alakesa was present, and ordered a measure of it to be at once shelled and cooked. The coming in of the carts and the king's order so exactly coincided with Kâlî's words that the Minister began to fear that he was quite unequal to the task of averting the fatality; yet the recollection of the smile of the goddess inspired him with fresh resolution, and he at once went to the palace-kitchen and requested the servants to inform him when the king was about to go to dinner. After issuing orders for the storing of the grain, king Alakesa retired to perform his morning ablutions and other religious duties.

Meanwhile a carriage containing the jars of sweetmeats sent by the king of Vijayanagara drove up to the palace, and the emissary who accompanied the present, told the royal servants that his master had commanded him to deliver it to king Alakesa in person. The First Minister well understood the meaning of this, and, promising to bring the king, went into the palace, caused one of the servants to be dressed like Alakesa, and conducted him to the carriage. The officer of the Vijayanagara king placed the first jar before the supposed Alakesa, who at once opened it, when lo! there darted forth several arrows, one of which pierced his heart, and he fell dead on the spot.[70] In an instant the emissary was seized and bound, and the officers began to lament the death of their good king. But the fatal occurrence spread rapidly through the palace, and soon the real Alakesa made his appearance on the scene. The officers now beheld one Alakesa dead and fallen to

[69] A *ghaṭikâ* = 24 minutes.—*T.*

[70] Apparently the arrows were attached to some kind of mechanism which discharged them on the opening of the jar. There is "nothing new under the sun." Dynamite is

the ground, pierced by the arrow, and another standing there alive and well. The First Minister then related how, suspecting treachery, he brought out a servant of the palace dressed like the king, and how he had been slain in place of his royal master. Alakesa thanked the Minister for having so ingeniously saved his life, and went into the palace. Thus was one of the three calamities to the king averted by the faithful Bodhaditya.

When it was the hour for dinner, the king and his courtiers all sat down, with the exception of the First Minister, who remained standing, without having taken a leaf for his own use. The king, observing this, with a smile pointed out a leaf to him,[71] but Bodhaditya would not sit; he wished to be near the king and to abstain from eating on that occasion. So the king allowed him to have his own way. The food having been served on the leaves, the hands of all, including the king, were mingling the rice, *ghî*, and *dhâl* for the first course. Near the king stood his faithful Minister Bodhaditya, and, when the king raised the first handful to his mouth, "Stop, my master," cried he, "I have long hoped for this handful as a present to me from your royal hands. I pray you give it to me, and feast upon the rest of the rice on your leaf."

This was uttered more in a tone of command than of request, and the king was highly incensed at what he naturally considered as insolence on the part of the Minister. For such a request, especially when made to a king, is deemed nothing less than an insult, while to refuse it is equally offensive. So, whatever thoughts may have passed through Alakesa's mind, recollecting how the Minister had that morning saved his life, he gave him the handful of rice, which Bodhaditya received with delight, feeling grateful for the favour of the goddess in being the means of averting this second calamity.

Far different, however, were the sentiments of the king and the assembled company. One and all declared Bodhaditya to be an insolent, proud fellow; but the king, while secretly blaming himself for having allowed him to use so much familiarity, suppressed his anger, in consideration of the important service the Minister had rendered him.

On the approach of night the heart of the First Minister throbbed violently, for the third calamity predicted by the goddess was yet to be encountered. His watch being ended, before retiring to rest, he went to examine the royal bedroom, where he saw the light burning brightly, and the king and queen asleep side by side in the ornamented swing cot, which was suspended from the roof by four chains. Presently, he perceived, with horror, a fierce black snake, the smell of which is enough to kill a man, slowly gliding down the chain near the head of the queen. The Minister noiselessly went forward, and with a single stroke of his sharp sword, cut the venomous brute in two. Bodhaditya, to avoid disturbing any person at such an hour of the night, threw the pieces over the canopy of the bed, rejoicing at having thus averted the third and last calamity. But a fresh horror then

perhaps a discovery of our own times, but "infernal machines," which served the purpose of king-killers, are of ancient date.

[71] The Hindûs, at their meals, squat on the ground, with leaves in place of earthenware dishes, on which their food is served.—*T.*

met his eyes; a drop of the snake's poison had fallen on the bosom of the queen, which was exposed in the carelessness of slumber.

"Alas, sacred goddess," he muttered, "why do you thus raise up new obstacles in my efforts to avert the evil which you predicted? I have done what I could to save the king, and in this last attempt I have killed his beloved queen. What shall I do?"

Having thus briefly reflected, he wiped off the poison from the queen's bosom with the tip of his little finger, and, lest the contact of the venom with his finger should endanger his own life, he cut the tip of it off and threw it on the canopy. Just then the queen awoke, and perceiving a man hastily leaving the room, she cried: "Who are you?"

The Minister respectfully answered: "Most venerable mother! I am your son, Bodhaditya," and at once retired.

Upon this the queen thought within herself: "Alas! is there such a thing as a good man in the world? Hitherto I have regarded this Bodhaditya as my son; but now he has basely taken the opportunity of thus disgracing me when my lord and I were sound asleep. I shall inform the king of this, and have that wretch's head struck off before the morning."

Accordingly she gently awakened the king, and with tears trickling down her beauteous face, she told him what had occurred, and concluded with these words:—"Till now, my lord, I considered that I was wife to you alone; but this night your First Minister has made me doubt it, since to my question, 'Who are you?' he answered, without any shame, 'I am Bodhaditya,' and went away."

On hearing of this violation of the sanctity of his bedchamber, Alakesa was greatly enraged, and determined to put to death such an unprincipled servant, but first to communicate the affair to his three other Ministers.

# CHAPTER XIII.

## SECOND PART.

When the Second Minister's watch was over, he went to inspect the guard at the royal bedchamber, and Alakesa hearing his footsteps inquired who was there.

"Your servant, Bodhachandra, most royal lord," was the reply.

"Enter, Bodhachandra," said the king; "I have somewhat to communicate to you."

Then Alakesa, almost choking with rage, told him of the gross offence of which his colleague the First Minister had been guilty, and demanded to know whether any punishment could be too severe. Bodhachandra humbled himself before the king, and thus replied—

"My lord, such a crime merits a heavy requital. Can one tie up fire in one's cloth and think that as it is but a small spark it will do us no harm? How, then, can we excuse even slight deviations from the rules of propriety? Therefore, if Bodhaditya be really guilty, he must be signally punished. But permit me to represent to your Majesty the advisability of carefully inquiring into this matter before proceeding to judgment. We ought to ascertain what reasons he had for such a breach of the harem rules; for should we, carried away by anger, act rashly in this affair, we may repent when repentance is of no avail. As an example, I shall, with your Majesty's permission relate a story." The king having at once given his consent, the Second Minister began to relate the

# STORY OF THE HONEST BUT RASH HUNTER AND HIS FAITHFUL DOG.

There dwelt in a certain forest a hunter named Ugravira, who was lord of the woods, and as such, had to pay a fixed sum of money to the king of the country. It happened once that the king unexpectedly demanded of him one thousand five hundred *pons*.[72] The hunter sold all his property and realised only a thousand *pons*, and was perplexed how to procure the rest of the required amount. At length he bethought him of his dog, which was of the best kind, and was beloved by him more than anything else in the whole world. He took his dog to an adjacent city, where he pledged him to a merchant named Kubera for five hundred *pons*, at the same time giving the merchant his bond for the loan. Before going away, the hunter with tears in his eyes, thus addressed the intelligent animal:—

"Mrigasimha, [*i.e.*, lion among beasts] O my faithful friend, do not leave thy new master until I have paid him back the money I have borrowed of him. Obey and serve him, even as thou hast ever obeyed and served me."

Some time after this, the merchant Kubera had to leave home and proceed with his merchandise to foreign countries: so he called the hunter's dog to his side, and bade him watch at his doors and prevent the intrusion of robbers and other evil-disposed persons. The dog indicated, both by his eyes and his tail, that he perfectly understood his instructions. Then the merchant, having enjoined his wife to feed the dog three times every day with rice and milk, set out on his travels. The dog kept his watch outside the house, and for a few days the merchant's wife fed him regularly three times a day. But this kind treatment was not to continue. She had for her paramour a wicked youth of the Setti caste, who, soon after the departure of Kubera, became a constant visitor at the merchant's house. The faithful dog instinctively surmised that his new master would not approve of such conduct; so one night, when the youth was leaving the house, Mrigasimha sprang upon him like an enraged lion, and seizing him by the throat, sent the evildoer to the other world. The merchant's wife hearing the scuffle, ran to the spot to save her lover, but found him dead.

Though extremely grieved at the loss of her paramour, she had the presence of mind to immediately carry the body to the garden at the back of the house, where she concealed it in a great pit, and covered it with earth and leaves, vainly thinking that she had thus concealed her own shame. All this was not done, however, without being observed by the watchful dog; and, henceforward, the merchant's wife

[72] A sum of money varying in different localities of the South of India. In the Chola grants "*pon*" also occurs.

hated him with a deadly hatred. She no longer gave him food, and the poor creature was fain to eat such grains of rice as he found adhering to the leaves thrown out of the house after meals, still keeping guard at the door.

After an absence of two months the merchant returned, and the dog, the moment he saw him, ran up to him and rolled himself on the ground at his feet; then seizing the merchant's cloth he dragged him to the very spot in the garden where the youth's body was hidden, and began to scratch the ground, at the same time looking into the merchant's face and howling dismally, from which Kubera concluded that the dog wished him to examine the place. Accordingly he dug up the spot and discovered the body of the youth, whom, indeed, he had suspected of being his wife's paramour. In a great fury he rushed into the house and commanded his wife, on pain of instant death, to relate the particulars of this affair without concealing anything. The wretched woman, seeing that her sin was discovered, confessed all, upon which her husband exclaimed!—

"Disgrace of womankind! you have not a fraction of the virtue possessed by this faithful brute, which you have, out of revenge, allowed to starve. But why should I waste words on thee? Happy am I in having no children by thee! Depart, and let me see thy face no more." So saying, he thrust her out of the house. Then the merchant fed the dog with milk, rice and sugar, after which he said to that lion of beasts (Mrigasimha, as he was called)—

"Thou trusty friend, language fails to express my gratitude to thee. The five hundred *pons* which I lent thy old master the hunter are as nothing compared with thy services to me, by which I consider the debt as more than paid. What must be the feelings of the hunter without thy companionship? I now give thee leave to return to him."

The merchant took the hunter's bond, and tearing it slightly at the top as a token that it was cancelled, he placed it in the dog's mouth and sent him back to his former master, and he at once set off towards the forest.

Now by this time the hunter had contrived to save up the five hundred *pons*, and with the money and the interest due thereon, he was going to the merchant to redeem his bond and reclaim his dog. To his great surprise he met Mrigasimha on the way, and as soon as the dog perceived him he ran up to him to receive his caresses. But the hunter immediately concluded that the poor brute, in his eagerness to rejoin him, had run away from the merchant, and determined to put him to death. Accordingly he plucked a creeper, and fastening it round the dog's neck tied him to a branch of a tree, and the faithful creature, who was expecting nothing but kindness from his old master, was by him most cruelly strangled. The hunter then continued his journey, and, on reaching the merchant's house, he laid down the money before him.

"My dear friend," said Kubera, "the important service your dog rendered me in killing my wife's paramour, has amply repaid your debt, so I gave him permission to return to you, with your bond in his mouth. Did you not meet him on your way? But why do you look so horrified? What have you done to the dog?"

The hunter, to whom everything was now only too clear, threw himself on the ground, like a huge tree cut at the root, and, after telling Kubera how he had inconsiderately slain the faithful dog, stabbed himself with his dagger. The merchant grieved at the death both of the dog and the hunter, which would not have occurred had he waited until Ugravira came to redeem his bond, snatched the weapon out of the hunter's breast and also stabbed himself. The news of this tragedy soon reached the forest, and the wife of the hunter, not wishing to survive her lord, threw herself into a well and was drowned. Lastly, even the wife of the merchant, finding that so many fatalities were due to her own misconduct, and that she was despised by the very children in the streets, put an end to her wretched life.

"Thus," added the Second Minister, "five lives were lost in consequence of the hunter's rashness. Wherefore I would respectfully beseech your Majesty to investigate the case of Bodhaditya, and to refrain from acting merely under the influence of anger."

Having thus spoken, Bodhachandra obtained leave to retire to his own house.

# CHAPTER XIII.

## THIRD PART.

At the end of the third watch of the night, Bodhavyapaka, the Third Minister of king Alakesa, went to see whether the royal bedchamber was properly guarded, and the king, summoning him to his presence, told him of the First Minister's crime, upon which Bodhavyapaka, after making due obeisance, thus spake:—

"Most noble king, such a grave crime should be severely punished, but it behoves us not to act before having ascertained that he is guilty beyond doubt, for evil are the consequences of precipitation, in proof of which I know a story which I will relate, with your Majesty's leave."

# STORY OF THE BRÂHMAṆ'S WIFE AND THE MUNGOOSE.

On the banks of the Ganges, which also flows by the most holy city of Banaras, there is a town named Mithila, where dwelt a very poor Brâhmaṇ called Vidyadhara. He had no children, and to compensate for this want, he and his wife tenderly nourished in their house a mungoose—a species of weasel. It was their all in all—their younger son, their elder daughter—their elder son, their younger daughter, so fondly did they regard that little creature. The god Visvesvara and his spouse Visalakshi observed this, and had pity for the unhappy pair; so by their divine power they blessed them with a son. This most welcome addition to their family did not alienate the affections of the Brâhmaṇ and his wife from the mungoose; on the contrary, their attachment increased, for they believed that it was because of their having adopted the pet that a son had been born to them. So the child and the mungoose were brought up together, as twin brothers, in the same cradle.

It happened one day when the Brâhmaṇ had gone out to beg alms of the pious and charitable, that his wife went into the garden to cull some pot-herbs, leaving the child asleep in his cradle, and by his side the mungoose kept guard. An old serpent, which was living in the well in the garden, crept into the house and under the cradle, and was beginning to climb into it to bite the child when the mungoose fiercely attacked it and tore it into several pieces, thus saving the life of the Brâhmaṇ's little son, and the venomous snake, that came to slay, itself lay dead beneath the cradle.

Pleased at having performed such an exploit, the mungoose ran into the garden to show the Brâhmaṇ's wife its blood-smeared mouth, but she rashly mistook the deliverer of her child for his destroyer, and with one stroke of the knife in her hand with which she was cutting herbs she killed the faithful creature, and then hastened into the house to see her dead son. But there she found the child in his cradle alive and well, only crying at the absence of his little companion, the mungoose, and under the cradle lay the great serpent cut to pieces. The real state of affairs was now evident, and the Brâhmaṇ presently returning home, his wife told him of her rash act and then put an end to her life. The Brâhmaṇ, in his turn, disconsolate at the death of the mungoose and his wife, first slew his child and then killed himself.

"And thus," added the Third Minister, "by one rash act four creatures perished, so true is it that precipitation results in a series of calamities. Do not, then, condemn Bodhaditya before his guilt is clearly proved." Alakesa, having given Bodhachandra the signal to retire, he quitted the presence and went home.

When the watch of the Fourth Minister, Bodhavibhishana, was terminated, he visited the private apartments of the king (who had been meanwhile pondering over the stories he had heard), and was called into the sleeping chamber by Alakesa, and informed of his colleague's unpardonable offence. The Minister, after due prostration, thus addressed his royal master:—

"Great king, I can scarcely bring myself to believe that Bodhaditya could ever be guilty of such a crime, and I would respectfully remind your Majesty that it would not be consistent with your world-wide reputation for wisdom and justice were you to pronounce judgment in this case without having inquired into all the circumstances. Evil and injustice result from hasty decisions and actions, of which a striking illustration is furnished in the

# STORY OF THE FAITHLESS WIFE AND THE UNGRATEFUL BLIND MAN.

In the town of Mithila there lived a young Brâhmaṇ who, having had a quarrel with his father-in-law, set out on a pilgrimage to Banaras. Going through a forest he met a blind man, whose wife was leading him by means of a stick, one end of which she held in her hand, and her husband holding the other end was following her. She was young and fair of face, and the pilgrim made signs to her that she should go with him and leave her blind husband behind. The proposal thus signified pleased this wanton woman, so she bade her husband sit under a tree for a few minutes while she went and plucked him a ripe mango. The blind man sat down accordingly, and his wife went away with the Brâhmaṇ. After waiting a long time in expectation of his wife's return, and no person coming near him, (for it was an unfrequented place), her infidelity became painfully apparent to him, and he bitterly cursed both her and the villain who had enticed her away from him. For six days he remained at the foot of the tree, in woeful condition, without a morsel of rice or a drop of water, and he was well nigh dead, when at length he heard the sound of footsteps near him, and cried faintly for help. A man of the Setti caste and his wife came up to him, and inquired how he happened to be in such a plight. The blind man told them how his wife had deserted him, and gone away with a young Brâhmaṇ whom they had met, leaving him there alone and helpless. His story excited the compassion of the Setti and his wife. They gave him to eat of the small quantity of rice they had with them, and, having supplied him with water to quench his thirst, the Setti bade his wife lead him with his stick. The woman, though somewhat reluctant to walk thus in company with a man who was not her husband, yet, reflecting that charitable actions ought never to be left undone, complied with her lord's request, and began to lead the blind man. After travelling in this manner for a day, the three reached a town, and took up their abode for the night in the house of a friend of the Setti, where the latter and his wife gave the blind man a share of their rice before tasting a morsel themselves. At daybreak the next morning they advised him to try to provide for himself in some way in that town, and prepared to resume their journey. But the blind man, forgetting all the kindness they had shown him, began to raise an alarm, crying out:—

"Is there no king in this city to protect me and give me my rights? Here is a Setti rascal taking away my wife with him! As I am blind, she denies that I am her husband, and follows that rogue! But will not the king give me justice?"

The people in the street at once reported these words to the king, who caused inquiry to be made into the matter. The fact of the Setti's wife having led the blind man, seemed to indicate that the latter, and not the Setti, was the woman's husband, and foolishly concluded that both the Setti and his wife were the real criminals. Accordingly he sentenced the Setti to the gallows, because he attempted to entice away a married woman, and his wife to be burnt in the kiln, as she wished to forsake her husband, and he a blind man. When these sentences were pronounced the blind man was thunder-struck. The thought that by a deliberate lie he had caused the death of two innocent persons now stung him to the heart. By this lie he expected that the Setti only should be punished, and that his wife would be made over to him as his own wife, but now he found she also was condemned to death.

"Vile wretch that I am!" said he; "I do not know what sins I committed in my former life to be thus blind now. My real wife, too, deserted me; and I, heaping sins upon sins, have now by a false report sent to death an innocent man and his wife, who rescued me from a horrible fate and tended to all my wants last night. O, Mahêśvara! what punishment you have in reserve for me I know not."

This soliloquy, being overheard by some by-standers, was communicated to the king, who bitterly reproaching himself for having acted so rashly, at once released the good Setti and his wife, and caused the ungrateful blind man to be burnt in the kiln.

"Thus, you see, my lord," added the fourth Minister, "how nearly that king had plunged himself into a gulf of crime by his rashness. Therefore, my most noble king, I would respectfully and humbly request you to consider well the case of Bodhaditya, and punish him severely if he be found really guilty."

Having thus spoken, the Fourth Minister obtained leave to depart.

# CHAPTER XIII.

## FOURTH PART.

The night was now over: darkness, the harbourer of vice, fled away; the day dawned. King Alakesa left his bedchamber, bathed and made his religious ablutions, and, after breakfasting, summoned a council of all his father's old ministers and advisers. Alakesa took his seat in the midst of the assembly; anger was clearly visible in his countenance; his eyes had lost their natural expression and had turned very red; his breath was as hot as that of a furnace. He thus addressed them:—

"Know ye all, the ministers of my father and of myself, that last night, during the first watch, my First Minister, Bodhaditya, while I and my queen were asleep in our chamber, came and touched with his finger the bosom of my queen. Consider well the gravity of this crime, and express your opinions as to what punishment he merits."

Thus spake king Alakesa, but all the ministers, not knowing what answer to return, hung down their heads in silence. Among those present was an aged minister named Manuniti, who called Bodhaditya to his side and privately learned the whole story. He then humbly bowed before the king, and thus spake:—

"Most noble king, men are not always all-wise, and, before replying to your Majesty's question, I beg permission to relate in your presence the story of a king in whose reign a certain benevolent action was repaid with disgrace and ignominy:—

# STORY OF THE WONDERFUL MANGO FRUIT.

On the banks of the Kâvêrî there was a city called Tiruvidaimarudur, where ruled a king named Chakraditya. In that city there lived a poor Brâhmaṇ and his wife, who, having no children, brought up in their house a young parrot as tenderly as if it had been their own offspring. One day the parrot was sitting on the roof of the house, basking itself in the morning sun, when a large flock of parrots flew past, talking to each other about certain mango fruits. The Brâhmaṇ's parrot asked them what were the peculiar properties of those fruits, and was informed that beyond the seven oceans there was a great mango tree, the fruit of which gave perpetual youth to the person who ate of it, however old and infirm he might be. On hearing of this wonder the Brâhmaṇ's parrot requested permission to accompany them, which being granted, they all continued their flight. When at length they arrived at the mango tree, all ate of its fruit; but the Brâhmaṇ's parrot reflected:—

"It would not be right for me to eat this fruit; I am young, while my adopted parents, the poor Brâhmaṇ and his wife are very old. So I shall give them this fruit, and they will become young and blooming by eating it."

And that same evening the good parrot brought the fruit to the Brâhmaṇ, and explained to him its extraordinary properties. But the Brâhmaṇ thought within himself:—

"I am a beggar. What matters it if I become young and live for ever, or else die this very moment? Our king is very good and charitable. If such a great man should eat of this fruit and renew his youth, he would confer the greatest benefit on mankind. Therefore I will give this mango to our good king."

In pursuance of this self-denying resolution, the poor Brâhmaṇ proceeded to the palace and presented the fruit to the king, at the same time relating how he had obtained it and its qualities. The king richly rewarded the Brâhmaṇ for his gift, and sent him away. Then he began to reflect thus:—

"Here is a fruit which can bestow perpetual youth on the person who eats it. I should gain this great boon for myself alone, and what happiness could I expect under such circumstances unless shared by my friends and subjects? I shall therefore not eat this mango-fruit, but plant it carefully in my garden, and it will in time become a tree, which will bear much fruit having the same wonderful virtue, and my subjects shall, every one, eat of the fruit, and, with myself, be endowed with everlasting youth."

So, calling his gardener, the king gave him the fruit, and he planted it in the royal presence. In due course of time the fruit grew into a fine tree, and during the spring season it began to bud and blossom and bear fruit. The king, having fixed upon an auspicious day for cutting one of the mango-fruits, gave it to his domestic chaplain, who was ninety years old, in order that his youth should be renewed. But no sooner had the priest tasted it than he fell down dead. At this unexpected calamity the king was both astonished and deeply grieved. When the old priest's wife heard of her husband's sudden death she came and prayed the king to allow her to perform *sati* with him on the same funeral pyre, which increased the king's sorrow; but he gave her the desired permission, and himself superintended all the ceremonies of the cremation. King Chakraditya then sent for the poor Brâhmaṇ, and demanded of him how he had dared to present a poisonous fruit to his king. The Brâhmaṇ replied:—

"My lord, I brought up a young parrot in my house, in order to console me for having no son. That parrot brought me the fruit one day, and told me of its wonderful properties. Believing that the parrot spoke the truth, I presented it to your Majesty, never for a moment suspecting it to be poisonous."

The king listened to the poor Brâhmaṇ's words, but thought that the poor priest's death should be avenged. So he consulted his ministers who recommended, as a slight punishment, that the Brâhmaṇ should be deprived of his left eye. This was done accordingly, and, on his return home, when his wife saw his condition, she asked the reason of such mutilation.

"My dear," said she, "the parrot we have fostered so tenderly is the cause of this."

And they resolved to break the neck of the treacherous bird. But the parrot, having overheard their conversation, thus addressed them:—

"My kind foster parents, everyone must be rewarded for the good actions or punished for the evil deeds of his previous life. I brought you the fruit with a good intention, but my sins in my former life have given it a different effect. Therefore I pray you to kill me and bury me with a little milk in a pit. And, after my funeral ceremony is over, I request you to undertake a pilgrimage to Banaras to expiate your own sins."

So the old Brâhmaṇ and his wife killed their pet parrot and buried it as directed, after which, overcome with grief, they set out on a pilgrimage to the Holy City.

Meanwhile the king commanded his gardener to set guards over the poison-tree, and to allow no one to eat of its fruit; and all the inhabitants soon came to know that the king had a mango tree in his garden, the fruit of which was deadly poison. Now, there was in the city an old washerwoman, who had frequent quarrels with her daughter-in-law, and one day, being weary of life, she left the house, threatening to eat of the poison tree and die.

The young parrot who was killed for having brought the poisonous mango-fruit was re-born as a green parrot, and was waiting for an opportunity to demonstrate the harmless nature of the tree; and when he saw the old woman approach with a determination to put an end to her life by eating of its fruit, he plucked one with his beak and dropped it down before her. The old woman rejoiced that fate sanctioned her death, and greedily ate the fruit, when lo! instead of dying she became young and blooming again. Those who had seen her leave the house a woman over sixty years of age were astonished on seeing her return as a handsome girl of sixteen and learning that the wonderful transformation was caused by the supposed poisonous mango-tree.

The strange news soon reached the king, who, in order to test the tree still further, ordered another fruit of it to be brought and gave it to a goldsmith of more than ninety years of age, who had embezzled some gold which had been entrusted to him to make into ornaments for the ladies of the palace, and was on that account undergoing imprisonment. When he had eaten the fruit, he, in his turn, became a young man of sixteen. The king was now convinced that the fruit of the mango-tree, so far from being poisonous, had the power of converting decrepit age into lusty and perennial youth. But how had the old priest died by eating of it?

It was by a mere accident. One day a huge serpent was sleeping on a branch of the mango-tree, and its head hung over one of the fruit; poison dropped from its mouth and fell on the rind of that fruit; the gardener, who had no knowledge of this, when asked to bring a fruit for the priest, happened to bring the one on which the poison had fallen, and the priest having eaten it, died.

And now the king caused proclamation to be made throughout his kingdom that all who pleased might come and partake of the mango-fruit, and everyone ate of it and became young. But king Chakaraditya's heart burnt within him at the remembrance of his ill-treatment of the poor Brâhmaṇ, who had returned with his wife from Banaras. So he sent for him, explained his mistake, and gave him a fruit to eat, which, having tasted, the aged Brâhmaṇ became young and his eye was also restored to him. But the greatest loss of all, that of the parrot who brought the fruit from beyond the seven oceans, remained irreparable.

"Thus, my lord," continued the old minister, Manuniti, "it behoves us not to act precipitately in this affair of Bodhaditya, which we must carefully sift before expressing our opinion as to the punishment he may deserve at your majesty's hands."

# CHAPTER XIII.

## FIFTH PART.

When Manuniti had concluded his story of the wonderful mango-fruit, king Alakesa ordered his four ministers to approach the throne, and then, with an angry countenance he thus addressed Bodhaditya:—

"What excuse have you for entering my bedchamber without permission, thus violating the rules of the harem?"

Bodhaditya humbly begged leave to relate to his majesty a story of how a Brâhmaṇ fed a hungry traveller and had afterwards to endure the infamy of having caused that traveller's death, and on king Alakesa signifying his consent, he thus began:—

# STORY OF THE POISONED FOOD.

There was a city called Vijayanagara, to the north of which flowed a small river with mango topes[73] on both banks. One day a young Brâhmiṇ pilgrim came and sat down to rest by the side of the stream, and, finding the place very cool and shady, he resolved to bathe, perform his religious ablutions, and make his dinner off the rice which he carried tied up in a bundle.

Three days before there had come to the same spot an old Brâhmiṇ whose years numbered more than three score and ten; he had quarrelled with his family, and had fled from his house to die. Since he had reached that place he had tasted no food, and the young pilgrim found him lying in a pitiable state, and placed near him a portion of his rice. The old man arose, and proceeded to the rivulet in order to wash his feet and hands, and pronounce a holy incantation or two before tasting the food.

While thus engaged a kite, carrying in its beak a huge serpent, alighted upon the tree at the foot of which was the rice given by the pilgrim to the old man, and while the bird was feasting on the serpent some of its poison dropped on the rice, and the old Brâhmiṇ, in his hunger, did not observe it on his return; he greedily devoured some of the rice, and instantly fell down dead.

The young pilgrim, seeing him prostrate on the ground, ran to help him, but found that life was gone; and concluding that the old man's hasty eating after his three days' fast must have caused his death, and being unwilling to leave his corpse to be devoured by kites and jackals, he determined to cremate it before resuming his journey. With this object he ran to the neighbouring village, and, reporting to the people what had occurred on the tope, requested their assistance in cremating the old man's body.

The villagers, however, suspected that the young pilgrim had killed and robbed the old Brâhmiṇ; so they laid hold of him, and, after giving him a severe flogging, imprisoned him in the village temple of Kâlî. Alas! what a reward was this for his kind hospitality! and how was he repaid for his beneficence!

The unhappy pilgrim gave vent to his sorrows in the form of verses in praise of the goddess in whose temple he was a prisoner; for he was a great Paṇḍit, versed in the four *Vêdas*, and the six *Śâstras*, and the sixty-four varieties of knowledge. On hearing the pilgrim's verses, the rage of the goddess descended upon the villagers, who had so rashly accused and punished him for a crime of which he was innocent. Suddenly the whole village was destroyed by fire, and the people lost all their property, and were houseless. In their extremity they went to the temple of Kâlî, and humbly requested the goddess to inform them of the cause of the calam-

[73] An Indian word meaning clumps of trees.

ity which had thus unexpectedly come upon them. The goddess infused herself into the person of one of the villagers, and thus responded:—

"Know ye, unkind villagers, that ye have most unjustly scourged and imprisoned in our presence an innocent, charitable, and pious Brâhmiṇ. The old man died from the effects of the poison, which dropped from a serpent's mouth on some rice at the foot of a tree when it was being devoured by a kite. Ye did not know of this; nevertheless ye have maltreated a good man without first making due inquiry as to his guilt or innocence. For this reason we visited your village with this calamity. Beware, and henceforward avoid such sins."

So saying, Kâlî departed from the person through whom she had manifested herself.[74] Then the villagers perceived the grievous error into which they had fallen. They released the good pilgrim and implored his forgiveness, which he readily granted. And thus was an innocent man charged with murder in return for his benevolent actions.

"Even so," continued Bodhaditya, "my most noble sovereign, I have this day had to endure the infamy of having violated the harem for saving your valuable life."

He then sent for a thief who was undergoing imprisonment, and gave him the handful of rice which he had the preceding day snatched from the king at dinner, and the thief having eaten it, instantly died. He next caused a servant to go to the royal bed-chamber, and fetch from the canopy of the couch the pieces of the serpent and his little finger-tip, which he laid before the wonder-struck king and the counsellors, and then addressed his majesty as follows:—

"My most noble king, and ye wise counsellors, it is known to you all that we four ministers keep watch over the town during the four quarters of the night, and mine is the first watch. Well, while I was on duty the day before yesterday, I heard a weeping voice in the direction of the temple. I proceeded to the spot, and discovered the goddess sobbing bitterly. She related to me how three calamities awaited the king on the morrow. The first of them was the arrows despatched by the king of Vijayanagara as sweetmeats to our Sovereign; the second was the poisoned rice, and the third the serpent. In trying to avert these calamities, I have committed the offence of entering the harem."

And he thereupon explained the whole affair from first to last.

King Alakesa and the whole assembly were highly delighted at the fidelity and devotion of Bodhaditya; for it was now very evident that he had done nothing amiss, but had saved the life of the king on three occasions, and indeed also the life of the queen by wiping off the serpent's poison which had fallen on her bosom. Then Alakesa related the following story in explanation of the proverb:—

[74] It is a very common practice to dupe the ordinary people in this manner in Hindu temples. Some impostor will proclaim to the crowd that the spirit of a god, or goddess, is upon him, and utters whatever comes uppermost in his mind. He occasionally contrives to accomplish his private ends by such "revelations." The ignorant are greatly misled by these impostors, and learned Hindus condemn the practice as gross superstition.—*T.*

# "EATING UP THE PROTECTOR."[75]

In the country of Uttara there lived a Brâhmiṇ named Kusalanatha, who had a wife and six sons. All lived in a state of prosperity for some time, but the entrance of Saturn into the Brâhmiṇ's horoscope turned everything upside down. The once prosperous Brâhmiṇ became poor, and was reduced to go to the neighbouring woods to gather bamboo rice with which to feed his hungry family.[76]

One day while plucking the bamboo ears, he saw a bush close by in flames, in the midst of which was a serpent struggling for its life. The Brâhmiṇ at once ran to its rescue, and stretching towards it a long green stick the reptile crept on to it and escaped from the flames, and then spread its hood and with a hissing sound approached to sting its rescuer. The Brâhmiṇ began to weep and bewail his folly in having saved the ungrateful creature, at which the serpent asked him:—

"O Brâhmiṇ, why do you weep?"

Said the old man: "You now purpose to kill me; is this the reward for my having saved your life?"

"True, you have rescued me from a terrible death, but how am I to appease my hunger?" replied the serpent.

And quoth the Brâhmiṇ, "You speak of your hunger, but who is to feed my old wife and six hungry children at my house?"

The serpent, seeing the anxiety of the Brâhmiṇ, emitted a precious gem from its hood, and bade him take it home and give it to his wife for household expenses, after which to return to the wood to be devoured. The old man agreed, and, solemnly promising to return without fail, went home. Having given the gem to his family, and told them of his pact with the serpent, the Brâhmiṇ went back to the wood. The serpent had meanwhile reflected upon its own base ingratitude.

"Is it right," said it to itself, "to kill him who saved me from the flames? No! I shall rather perish of hunger, if I cannot find a prey to-day, than slay my protector."

So when the old Brâhmiṇ appeared, true to his word, the serpent presented him with another valuable gem, and after expressing a wish that he should live long and happily with his wife and children, went its own way, while the Brâhmiṇ returned joyously to his home.

"Even as the serpent purposed acting towards its benefactor," continued the

[75] Corresponding to the English proverb: "Quarrelling with one's bread and butter."

[76] Full grown and ripe bamboo bears a kind of corn which when collected and shelled resembles wheat. Hunters cook a most excellent food of bamboo grain and honey.—*T.*

king, "so did I, in my rage, intend putting to death my faithful minister and the protector of my life, Bodhaditya; and to free myself from this grievous sin there is no penance I should not undergo."

Then king Alakesa ordered a thousand Brâhmiṇs to be fed every day during his life, and many rich gifts to be distributed in temples as atonement for his great error. And from that day Bodhaditya and his three colleagues enjoyed still more of the royal favour. With those four faithful ministers king Alakesa lived a most happy life and had a most prosperous reign.

May there be prosperity to all!

# CHAPTER XIV.

## THE MONKEY WITH THE TOM-TOM.[77]

In a remote wood there lived a monkey, and one day while he was eating wood-apples, a sharp thorn from the tree ran into the tip of his tail, he tried his best to get it out but could not. So he proceeded to the nearest village, and calling the barber asked him to oblige him by removing the thorn.

"Friend barber," said the monkey, "a thorn has run into my tail. Kindly remove it and I will reward you."

The barber took up his razor and began to examine the tail; but as he was cutting out the thorn he cut off the tip of the tail. The monkey was greatly enraged and said:—

"Friend barber, give me back my tail. If you cannot do that, give me your razor."

The barber was now in a difficulty, and as he could not replace the tip of the tail he had to give up his razor to the monkey.

The monkey, went back to the wood with his razor thus trickishly acquired. On the way he met an old woman, who was cutting fuel from a dried-up tree.

"Grandmother, grandmother," said the monkey, "the tree is very hard. You had better use this sharp razor, and you will cut your fuel easily."

The poor woman was very pleased, and took the razor from the monkey. In cutting the wood she, of course, blunted the razor, and the monkey seeing his razor thus spoiled, said:—

"Grandmother, you have spoiled my razor. So you must either give me your fuel or get me a better razor."

The woman was not able to procure another razor. So she gave the monkey her fuel and returned to her house bearing no load that day.

The roguish monkey now put the bundle of dry fuel on his head and proceeded to a village to sell it. There he met an old woman seated by the roadside and making puddings. Said the monkey to her:—

"Grandmother, grandmother, you are making puddings and your fuel is already exhausted. Use mine also and make more cakes."

---

[77] Compare the story of "The Rat's Wedding" from the Pañjâb, *The Indian Antiquary*, Vol. XI., pp, 226ff: where, however, a better moral from the tale is drawn.

The old lady thanked him for his kindness and used his fuel for her puddings. The cunning monkey waited till the last stick of his fuel was burnt up, and then he said to the old woman:—

"Grandmother, grandmother, return me my fuel or give me all your puddings."

She was unable to return him the fuel, and so had to give him all her puddings.

The monkey with the basket of puddings on his head walked and walked till he met a *Paraiya*[78] coming with a tom-tom towards him.

"Brother Paraiya," said the monkey, "I have a basketful of puddings to give you. Will you, in return, present me with your tom-tom?"

The *Paraiya* gladly agreed, as he was then very hungry, and had nothing with him to eat.

The monkey now ascended with the tom-tom to the topmost branch of a big tree and there beat his drum most triumphantly, saying in honour of his several tricks:—

"I lost my tail and got a razor; *ḍum ḍum.*"[79]

"I lost my razor and got a bundle of fuel; *ḍum ḍum.*"

"I lost my fuel and got a basket of puddings; *ḍum ḍum*".

"I lost my puddings and got a tom-tom; *ḍum ḍum.*"

Thus there are rogues in this innocent world, who live to glory over their wicked tricks.

[78] A low caste man; Pariah.

[79] In response to the sound of the tom-tom.

# CHAPTER XV.

## PRIDE GOETH BEFORE A FALL.

Corresponding to this English proverb, there is one in Tamil—*Ahambhâ vam âlai aḻikkum*—"Self-pride brings destruction;" and the following story is related by the common folk to illustrate it.

In a certain village there lived ten cloth merchants, who always went about together. Once upon a time they had travelled far afield, and were returning home with a great deal of money which they had obtained by selling their wares. Now there happened to be a dense forest near their village, and this they reached early one morning. In it there lived three notorious robbers, of whose existence the traders had never heard, and while they were still in the middle of it, the robbers stood before them, with swords and cudgels in their hands, and ordered them to lay down all they had. The traders had no weapons with them, and so, though they were many more in number, they had to submit themselves to the robbers, who took away everything from them, even the very clothes they wore, and gave to each only a small loin-cloth (*laṅgôṭî*), a span in breadth and a cubit in length.

The idea that they had conquered ten men, and plundered all their property, now took possession of the robbers' minds. They seated themselves like three monarchs before the men they had plundered, and ordered them to dance to them before returning home. The merchants now mourned their fate. They had lost all they had, except their chief essential, the *laṅgôṭî*, and still the robbers were not satisfied, but ordered them to dance.

There was, among the ten merchants, one who was very intelligent. He pondered over the calamity that had come upon him and his friends, the dance they would have to perform, and the magnificent manner in which the three robbers had seated themselves on the grass. At the same time he observed that these last had placed their weapons on the ground, in the assurance of having thoroughly cowed the traders, who were now commencing to dance. So he took the lead in the dance, and, as a song is always sung by the leader on such occasions, to which the rest keep time with hands and feet, he thus began to sing:—

*Nâmânum puli per,*
*Tâlanum tiru pêr:*
*Sâvana tâḷanai*
*Tiruvaṇan śuttinân,*
*Sâvana tâlan mîdi*
*Tâ tai tôm tadingaṇa.*

"We are *puli* men,
They are *tiru* men:
If one *śâ* man,
Surrounds *tiru* men.
*Śa* man remains.
*Tâ, tai, tôm, tadingaṇa.*"

The robbers were all uneducated, and thought that the leader was merely singing a song as usual. So it was in one sense; for the leader commenced from a distance, and had sung the song over twice, before he and his companions commenced to approach the robbers. They had understood his meaning, which, however, even to the best educated, unless trained to the technical expressions of trade, would have remained a riddle.

When two traders discuss the price of an article in the presence of a purchaser, they use an enigmatic form of language.

"What is the price of this cloth?" one trader will ask another.

"*Puli* rupees," another will reply, meaning "ten rupees."

Thus, there is no possibility of the purchaser knowing what is meant unless he be acquainted with trade technicalities.[80] By the rules of this secret language *tiru* means "three," *puli* means "ten," and *śâvana* (or shortly *śa*) means "one." So the leader by his song meant to hint to his fellow-traders that they were ten men, the robbers only three, that if three pounced upon each of the robbers, nine of them could hold them down, while the remaining one bound the robbers' hands and feet.

The three thieves, glorying in their victory, and little understanding the meaning of the song and the intentions of the dancers, were proudly seated chewing betel and *tambâk* (tobacco). Meanwhile the song was sung a third time. *Tâ tai tôm* had left the lips of the singer; and, before *tadingaṇa* was out of them, the traders separated into parties of three, and each party pounced upon a thief. The remaining one—the leader himself, for to him the other nine left the conclusion—tore up into long narrow strips a large piece of cloth, six cubits long, and tied the hands and feet of the robbers. These were entirely humbled now, and rolled on the ground like three bags of rice!

The ten traders now took back all their property, and armed themselves with the swords and cudgels of their enemies; and when they reached their village, they often amused their friends and relatives by relating their adventure.[81]

---

[80] Traders have also certain secret symbols for marking their prices on their cloths.

[81] This story, apart from its folklore value, is specially interesting as showing that the customs mentioned in the *Indian Antiquary*, Vol. XIV., pp. 155ff., as being prevalent at Delhi, regarding secret trade language are universal in India.

# CHAPTER XVI.

## GOOD WILL GROW OUT OF GOOD.

In a certain town there reigned a king named Patnîpriya,[82] to whose court, a poor old Brâhmiṇ, named Pâpabhîru,[83] came every morning, with a yellow lime in his hand, and presenting it to the king, pronounced a benediction in Tamil:—

*Nanmai vidaittâl, nanmai viḷaiyum:*
*Tîmai vidaittâl, tîmai vijaiyum:*
*Nanmaiyum tîmaiyum pinvara kâṇalâm.*

"If good is sown, then good will grow:
If bad is sown, then bad will grow:
Thus good or bad the end will show."

The king respected as much the noble benediction of the Brâhman as he did his grey hairs.

In this way the presentation of the fruit continued daily, though the Brâhmiṇ had nothing to request from the king, but simply wished to pay his respects. On observing that he had no ulterior motives, but was merely actuated by *râjasêvana*, or duty to his king, the king's admiration for his old morning visitor increased the more.

After presenting the fruit the Brâhmiṇ waited upon his sovereign till his *pûjâ*[84] was over, and then went home where his wife kept ready for him all the requisites for his own *pûjâ*. Pâpabhîru then partook of what dinner his wife had prepared for him. Sometimes, however, a Brâhmiṇ neighbour sent him an invitation to dinner, which he at once accepted. For his father, before he breathed his last, had called him to his bedside, and, pronouncing his last benediction, had thus advised him in Tamil:—

*Kâlai sôttai taḷḷâde,*
*Kaṇṇil Kaṇḍadai śollâde,*
*Râjanukku payandu naḍa."*

"Morning meal do thou never spurn,
Nor say thou what thine eyes discern,
But serve thy king for fame to earn."

Thus it was that Pâpabhîru began his visits to the king, nor did he ever reject an

[82] *i.e.,* lover of his wife.
[83] *i.e.,* a shudder at sin.
[84] Worship of the household gods or devotion.

invitation to dinner, though it might come at a very inconvenient time.

Now on a certain *êkâdaśi*[^°] morning, Pâpabhîru went to the king to pay his respects as usual, with the lime and the benediction, but found that he had gone to his *pûjâ* and so followed him there. On seeing the Brâhmiṇ, the king's face glowed with pleasure, and he said:—

"My most revered god on earth,[86] I thought that some ill must have befallen you, when I missed you in the council-hall this morning; but praised be Paramêśvara for having sent you to me, though it is a little late. I never do my *pûjâ* without placing my scimitar by the side of the god, but last night I left it in my queen's room. It is under the pillow of the couch on which I usually sleep. Until you came I could find no suitable person to fetch it for me, and so I have waited for you. Would you kindly take the trouble to fetch it for me?"

The poor Brâhmiṇ was only too glad of the opportunity thus presented to him of serving his king, and so he ran to the *harem* and into the room where the king usually slept. The queen was a very wicked woman and always having secret meetings with courtiers of her husband, so when Pâpabhîru returned he surprised the queen and one of her lovers walking in the garden, he went through, however, to the king's room, and lifting up the king's pillow felt for the scimitar, and went away. True however, to his father's words, "Nor say thou what thine eyes discern," he never opened his lips and went his way with a heavy heart.

The queen and her wicked suitor were greatly alarmed.

"That rogue of an old Brâhmiṇ has seen us and may report to the king at the first opportunity," faltered the minister.

But the queen, as bold in words as in sin, said; "I will have him murdered before the sun rises. Wait you here. I shall inform the king of what is to be done and report the result to you, and then you may go home."

So saying, she went and stood before her royal husband who was at his worship. Patnîpriya rose up and asked her the reason of her sudden appearance.

Said she, "Your Majesty seems to think the whole world as innocent as yourself. That wretched old Brâhmiṇ, though his hair is as white as milk, has not forgotten his younger days, he asked me to run away with him. If you do not order his death before to-morrow morning, I shall kill myself."

The king was much vexed with what he heard, and all the regard he had for the Brâhmiṇ disappeared at once. He called two of his executioners and spoke to them thus before his wife:—

"Take to the east gate of the town a large iron caldron, and keep it boiling to the brim with gingely oil.[87] A certain person shall come to you in the morning and ask you, 'Is it all done?' Without observing who he is, tie his hands and feet and

[85] The eleventh lunar day of every fortnight, on which a fast is observed by orthodox Hindûs.

[86] *Bhûsura, bhûdêva*; a generic name for a Brâhmiṇ.

[87] Oil of sesamun; *til* and gingely oil are the ordinary names for this common product of India.

throw him into the boiling oil. When he has been boiled to death, put out the fire and empty out the oil."

The executioners received the order and went away to perform their terrible duty. The queen, too, glad at heart at having thus successfully arranged for the murder of the Brâhmiṇ, reported the fact to the minister, but said nothing about the special question to be put by the victim. The minister, much pleased, went to his palace and waited for news of the Brâhmiṇ's death.

When his *pûjâ* was over the king sent for Pâpabhîru, and the poor Brâhmiṇ, never having before been sent for at such a time, made his appearance with a beating heart. When he arrived the king, in order to arouse no suspicion in his mind, said gently to him:—

"My dear Brâhmiṇ, to-morrow morning, when you go to make your ablutions, pass by the east gate. There you will see two persons seated by the side of a large caldron. Ask them, 'Is it all done?' And whatever reply they give you, come and communicate to me."

Thus spoke the king, firmly believing that Pâpabhîru would never return to him; while the Brâhmiṇ, glad to be able to serve the king a second time next morning, went home and slept soundly. Early in the morning, even a *ghaṭikâ* before his usual time, he got up, and, placing on his head a bag containing dry clothes, proceeded to the river for his morning bath. He took the road to the eastern gate as he had been ordered, but had not walked far when a friend invited him to a *dvâdaśi*[88] breakfast.

"My poor old mother did not taste even a drop of water the whole of the *êkâdaśi,* (yesterday). Rice and hot water for a bath are ready. Pour a little of the water over your head,[89] pronounce one *gâyatrî*[90] and taste a handful of rice. Whatever may be the urgency of your business, oblige me for my poor mother's sake."

Thus spoke his friend, and Pâpabhîru, out of regard to his father's order never to spurn a morning meal, ran in haste into his friend's house to oblige him; the king's order all the while sitting heavily on his mind.

Meanwhile the minister was most anxious to hear the news of the Brâhmiṇ's death, but was afraid to send any one to inquire about it, lest he should arouse suspicion. So he went himself to the east gate, as soon as the sun had risen, and asked the executioners, sitting by the side of the caldron, by way of a simple question: "Is the business all done?" And as they were instructed not to observe who the person was that came to question them, but to tie him up and boil him in the oil, they, notwithstanding his howls, bound him and threw him in. As soon as he was dead, they extinguished the fire, poured out the oil, turned over the caldron, corpse and all.

The Brâhmiṇ finished his *dvâdaśi* breakfast, in great haste, and, with the betel

[88] *Dvâdaśi* is the twelfth lunar day, on which early in the morning, before even the fifth *ghaṭikâ* is over, every orthodox Hindû is obliged by his religious codes to break the previous day's fast.

[89] Lit. a "chombu-full;" the *chombu* is a small vessel.

[90] A sacred hymn.

leaf still in his hand, ran to the gate to inquire of the persons seated by the caldron whether it was all done. When he put them the question, they smilingly replied:—

"Yes, Sir, it is all done. The minister is boiled to death. We gave full execution to the king's orders. You may go and report the affair to him."

The Brâhmiṇ, not knowing the reason for the course events had taken, ran back and reported the reply of the executioners to the king. The minister's interference in the affair at once kindled suspicion in the king's mind. He unsheathed his scimitar, and holding it in his right hand, twisted the lock of hair on the Brâhmiṇ's head into his left. He then asked him whether he had not tried to get his wife away from him the previous morning, and told him that, if he concealed the truth, he would make an end of him. The poor Brâhmiṇ now confessed what he had seen, on which the king threw down the scimitar and fell down on his knees before him.

"The words of thy benediction, O respected Brâhmiṇ, have only now been explained to me. Thou hast sown nothing but good; and good in having thy life preserved, hast thou reaped. The wicked minister—whose conscious guilt made him so very anxious to hear about thy death—because he sowed a bad intention in his heart has reaped evil, even a death that he never expected. Another victim of evil sowing, remains in my queen, in whom I placed an undeserved love."

So said he, and ordered her to the gallows. The old Brâhmiṇ he appointed his minister and reigned for a long time.

# CHAPTER XVII.

## LIGHT MAKES PROSPERITY.

There is a Tamil proverb *dîpam lakshmîkaram,* meaning, "light makes prosperity," and the following story is related to explain it:—

In the town of Gôvindapâthî there lived a merchant named Paśupati Śeṭṭi, who had a son and a daughter. The son's name was Vinîta and the daughter's Garvî, and while still playmates they made a mutual vow, that in case they ever had children that could be married to each other, they would certainly see that this was done. Garvî grew up to marry a very rich merchant, and gave birth in due course to three daughters, the last of whom was named Sunguṇî. Vinîta, too, had three sons. Before, however, this brother and sister could fulfil their vow an event happened which threw a gloom over all their expectations.

Paśupati Śeṭṭi died, and his creditors—for he had many—grew troublesome. All his property had to be sold to clear his debts, and in a month or two after his father's death Vinîta was reduced to the condition of a penniless pauper. But being a sensible person he patiently bore up against his calamity, and tried his best to live an honest life on what little was left to him.

His sister Garvî was, as has been already said, married into a rich family, and when she saw the penniless condition of her brother the engagements she had entered into with him began to trouble her. To give or not to give her daughters in marriage to the sons of her brother! This was the question that occupied her thoughts for several months, till at last she determined within herself never to give poor husbands to her children. Fortunately for her, two young merchants of respectable family offered themselves to her two eldest daughters, she gladly accepted them and had the weddings celebrated. The last daughter, Suguṇî, alone remained unmarried.

Vinîta was sorely troubled in his heart at this disappointment, as he never thought that his sister would thus look down upon his poverty; but, being very sensible, he never interfered and never said a word. The vow of his childhood was, however, known to every one, and some came to sympathise with him; while others spoke in a criticising tone to Garvî for having broken her promise, because her brother had become poor through unforeseen circumstances. Their remarks fell on the ears of Suguṇî, who was as yet unmarried, and also was a very learned and sensible girl. She found her uncle Vinîta extremely courteous and respectful, and his sons all persons of virtue and good nature. The thought that her mother should have forgotten all these excellent and rare qualities in the presence of fleeting mammon (*asthiraiśvarya*) vexed her heart very greatly. So, though it is considered most contrary to etiquette for a girl in Hindû society to fix upon a boy as her husband, she approached her mother and thus addressed her:—

"Mother, I have heard all the story about your vow to your brother to marry us—myself and my sisters—to his sons, our cousins; but I am ashamed to see you have unwarrantably broken it in the case of my sisters. I cannot bear such shame. I cannot marry anyone in the world except one of my three cousins. You must make up your mind to give me your consent."

Garvî was astonished to hear her youngest daughter talk thus to her.

"You wish to marry a beggar?" said she. "We will never agree to it, and if you persist we will give you away to your penniless pauper, but we will never see your face again."

But Suguṇî persisted. So her marriage with the youngest son of Vinîta was arranged. He had never spoken a word about it to his sister, but he had waited to make matches for his children till all his sister's daughters had been given away, and when he heard that Suguṇî was determined to marry his youngest son, he was very pleased. He soon fixed upon two girls from a poor family for his other sons, and celebrated the three weddings as became his position.

Suguṇî was as noble in her conduct as in her love for her poor cousin. She was never proud or insolent on account of having come from a rich family. Nor did she ever disregard her husband, or his brothers, or father.

Now Vinîta and his sons used to go out in the mornings to gather dried leaves which his three daughters-in-law stitched into plates (*patrâvalî*), which the male members of the family sold in the *bâzâr* for about four *paṇams* each.[91] Sometimes these leaf-plates would go for more, sometimes for less; but whatever money the father-in-law brought home his daughters-in-law used for the day's expense. The youngest of them was Suguṇî, who spent the money most judiciously, and fed her father-in-law and his sons sumptuously. Whatever remained she partook of with her two poor sisters-in-law, and lived most contentedly. And the family respected Suguṇî as a paragon of virtue, and had a very great regard for her. Her parents, as they had threatened, never returned to see how their last, and of course once beloved, child was doing in her husband's home. Thus passed a couple of years.

One day the king of the town was taking an oil bath, and pulling a ring off his finger, left it in a niche in the open courtyard. A *garuḍa* (Brâhmaṇî kite) was at that moment describing circles in the air, and, mistaking the glittering rubies in the ring for flesh, pounced upon it and flew away. Finding it not to be flesh he dropped it in the house of Suguṇî's husband. She happened to be alone working in the courtyard, while her sisters-in-law and the others were in different parts of the house. So she took up the sparkling ring and hid it in her lap.

Soon afterwards she heard a proclamation made in the street that the king had lost a valuable ring, and that any person who could trace it and give it back to him should obtain a great reward. Suguṇî called her husband and his brothers and thus

[91] A *paṇam* is generally worth two *ânâs*.

addressed them:—

"My lord and brothers, I have the king's ring. Exactly at midday a *garuḍa* dropped it in our courtyard and here it is. We must all go to the king, and there, before you three, I shall deliver up the ring, explaining how I got it. When his majesty desires me to name my reward I shall do so, and beg of you never to contradict or gainsay my desires, if they appear very humble in your opinion."

The brothers agreed, and they all started for the palace. They had a very great respect for Suguṇî and expected a good result from this visit to the king.

The palace was reached, and the ring was given back to the king with the explanation. His majesty was charmed at the modesty and truthfulness of Suguṇî, and asked her to name her reward.

"My most gracious sovereign! King of kings! Supreme lord! Only a slight favour thy dog of a servant requests of your majesty. It is this, that on a Friday night all the lights in the town be extinguished, and not a lamp be lit even in the palace. Only the house of thy dog of a servant must be lighted up with such lights as it can afford."

"Agreed, most modest lady. We grant your request, and we permit you to have the privilege you desire this very next Friday."

Joyfully she bowed before his majesty, and returned with her husband and the others to her house. She then pledged the last jewel she had by her and procured some money.

Friday came. She fasted the whole day, and as soon as twilight approached she called both the brothers of her husband, and thus addressed them:—

"My brothers, I have made arrangements for lighting up our house with one thousand lamps to-night. One of you, without ever closing your eyes for a moment, must watch the front of our house and the other the back. If a woman of a graceful appearance and of feminine majesty wishes you to permit her to enter it, boldly tell her to swear first never to go out again. If she solemnly agrees to this, then permit her to come in. If in the same way any woman wishes to go out, make a similar condition that she must swear never to return at any time in her life."

What Suguṇî said seemed ridiculous to the brothers; but they allowed her to have her way, and waited to see patiently what would take place.

The whole town was gloomy that night, except Suguṇî's house; for, by order of his majesty, no light was lit in any other house. The *Ashṭalakshmîs*—the Eight Prosperities—entered the town that night and went house by house into every street. All of them were dark, and the only house lit up was Suguṇî's. They tried to enter it, but the brother at the door stopped them and ordered them to take the oath. This they did, and when he came to understand that these ladies were the Eight Prosperities, he admired the sagacity of his brother's wife.

A *nimisha* after the eight ladies had gone in, there came out of the house a hideous female and requested permission to go, but the brother at the back would not permit this unless she swore never to come back again. She solemnly swore, and the next moment he came to know that she was *Mûdêvî*, or Adversity, the elder sister of Prosperity.

For she said:—"My sisters have come. I cannot stay here for a minute longer. God bless you and your people. I swear by everything sacred never to come back."

And so, unable to breathe there any longer, Adversity ran away.

When the morning dawned, the Prosperities had already taken up a permanent abode with the family. The rice bag became filled. The money chest overflowed with money. The pot contained milk. And thus plenty began to reign in Suguṇî's house from that day. The three brothers and her father-in-law were overjoyed at the way Suguṇî had driven away their poverty for ever, and even Suguṇî's parents did not feel it a disgrace to come and beg their daughter's pardon. She nobly granted it and lived with all the members of her family in prosperity for a long life.

It is a notion, therefore, among orthodox Hindûs, that light in the house brings prosperity, and darkness adversity.[92]

[92] See also the second tale in this series.

# CHAPTER XVIII.

## CHANDRALÊKHÂ AND THE EIGHT ROBBERS.

There was an ancient city named Kaivalyam, in the Pâṇḍiya country, and in that city there lived a dancing girl named Muttumôhanâ. She was an excellent gem of womankind, for though born of the dancing-girls' caste, she was a very learned and pious woman, and never would she taste her food without first going and worshipping in the temple of Śiva. She moved in the society of kings, ministers, and Brâhmiṇs, and never mingled with low people, however rich they might be. She had a daughter named Chandralêkhâ, whom she put to school with the sons of kings, ministers and Brâhmiṇs. Chandralêkhâ showed signs of very great intelligence, even when she was beginning her alphabet, so that the master took the greatest care with her tuition, and in less than four years she began her lessons and became a great *panditâ*.[93] However, as she was only a dancing-girl by birth, there was no objection to her attending to her studies in open school till she attained to maturity, and, accordingly, up to that age she attended the school and mastered the four *Vêdas* and *Śâstras* and the sixty-four varieties of knowledge.

She then ceased to attend the school, and Muttumôhanâ said to her:—

"My darling daughter, for the last seven or eight years you have been taking lessons under the Brâhmiṇ, your master, in the various departments of knowledge, and you must now pay a large fee to remunerate your master's labours in having taught you so much. You are at liberty to take as much money as you please from my hoard."

So saying she handed over the key to her daughter, and Chandralêkhâ, delighted at her mother's sound advice, filled up five baskets with five thousand *mohars* in each, and setting them on the heads of five maid-servants, went to her master's house with betel leaves, areca nut, flowers and cocoanuts in a platter in her hand, to be presented along with the money. The servants placed the baskets before the master and stood outside the house, while Chandralêkhâ took the dish of betel leaves, nuts, &c., and humbly prostrated herself on the ground before him. Then, rising up, she said:—

"My most holy *gurû* (master), great are the pains your holiness undertook in instructing me, and thus destroying the darkness of my ignorance. For the last eight years I have been a regular student under your holiness, and all the branches of knowledge hath your holiness taught me. Though what I offer might be insufficient for the pains your holiness took in my case, still I humbly request your

[93] Learned woman.

holiness to accept what I have brought."

Thus said she, and respectfully pushed the baskets of *mohars* and the betel-nut platter towards the Brâhmiṇ. She expected to hear benedictions from her tutor, but in that we shall see she was soon disappointed.

Replied the wretched Brâhmiṇ:—

"My dear Chandralêkhâ, do you not know that I am the tutor of the prince, the minister's son and several others of great wealth in Kaivalyam? Of money I have more than enough. I do not want a single *mohar* from you, but what I want is that you should marry me."[94]

Thus spoke the shameless teacher, and Chandralêkhâ's face changed colour. She was horrified to hear such a suggestion from one whom she had thought till then to be an incarnation of perfection. But, still hoping to convince him of the unjustness of the request, she said:—

"My most holy master! The deep respect I entertain towards your holy feet is such that, though your holiness's words are plain, I am led to think that they are merely uttered to test my character. Does not your holiness know the rules by which a preceptor is to be regarded as a father, and that I thus stand in the relationship of a daughter to your holiness? So kindly forget all that your holiness has said, and accepting what I have brought in my humble state, permit me to go home."

But the wretched teacher never meant anything of the sort. He had spoken in earnest, and his silence now and lascivious look at once convinced the dancing-girl's daughter of what was passing in his mind. So she quickly went out and told her servants to take back the money.

At home Muttumôhanâ was anxiously awaiting the return of her daughter, and as soon as Chandralêkhâ came in without the usual cheerfulness in her face, and without having given the presents, her mother suspected that something had gone wrong, and inquired of her daughter the cause of her gloom. She then related to her mother the whole story of her interview with her old master. Muttumôhanâ was glad to find such a firm heart in her daughter, and blessed her, saying that she would be wedded to a young husband, and lead a chaste life, though born of the dancing-girls' caste. The money she safely locked up in her room.

Now, the Brâhmiṇ, in consequence of his disappointment, was very angry with Chandralêkhâ, and, that no young and wealthy gentleman might visit her house, he spread reports that Chandralêkhâ was possessed of a demon (*kuṭṭîchchâtti*). So no one approached Chandralêkhâ's house to win her love, and her mother was much vexed. Her great wish was that some respectable young man should secure her daughter's affections, but the master's rumours stood in the way. And thus a year passed, and the belief that a *kuṭṭîchchâtti* had possessed Chandralêkhâ gained firm ground.

After what seemed to these two to be a long period, a sage happened to visit

[94] There would of course be no *real* marriage between a dancing girl and a Brâhmiṇ. Hence the insult.

Muttumôhanâ's house, and she related to him all her daughter's story. He listened and said:—

"Since the belief that a demon has taken possession of your daughter has taken firm hold of the citizens, it is but necessary now that she should perform (*pûjâ*) worship to the demon-king on the night of the new moon of this month in the cremation-ground. Let her do this and she will be all right, for then some worthy young man can secure her affections."

So saying the sage went away, and his advice seemed to be reasonable to the mother. She very well knew that no such demon had possessed her daughter, but that it was all the master's idle report. But still, to wipe away any evil notion in the minds of the people she publicly proclaimed that her daughter would perform *pûjâ* in the cremation-ground at midnight at the next new moon.[95] Now, it is always the rule in such rites that the person who is possessed should go alone to the cremation-ground, and, accordingly, on the night of the next new moon, Chandralêkhâ went to the burning-ground with a basket containing all the necessary things for worship, and a light.

Near Kaivalyam, at a distance of five *kôs* from it, was a great forest called *Khâṇḍavam*. In it there dwelt eight robbers, who used to commit the greatest havoc in the country round. At the time that Chandralêkhâ proceeded to the cremation-ground, these eight robbers also happened to go there to conceal what they had stolen in the earlier part of that night. Then, being relieved of their burden, they determined to go to some other place to plunder during the latter half of the night also. When Chandralêkhâ heard the sound of footsteps at a distance she feared something wrong, and, covering up her glittering light by means of her empty basket, concealed herself in a hollow place. The thieves came and looked round about them. They found nobody, but, fearing that some one might be near, one of them took out an instrument called *kannakkôl*, and, whirling it round his head, threw it towards the east. This *kannakkôl* is the instrument by which these robbers bore holes in walls and enter buildings, and some robbers say they get it from a thunderbolt. During a stormy day they make a large heap of cow-dung, into which a thunderbolt falls and leaves a rod in the middle, which is so powerful that it can bore even through stone walls without making any noise. It has also the attribute of obeying its master's orders. So when the chief of the eight robbers threw his *kannakkôl* towards the east, true to its nature, it fell into the hole in which Chandralêkhâ was hiding, and began to pierce her in the back. As soon as she felt it, she dragged it out by both her hands without making the slightest noise, and, throwing it under her feet, stood firmly over it. The robbers, having concealed the eight boxes of wealth they had brought with them in the sands near the cremation-ground, went away to spend the remaining part of the night usefully in their

[95] In stories of a master falling in love with the girl he has been teaching, he is usually himself made a soothsayer. In that capacity he asks the guardian (father or mother) to put the girl in a light box and to float her down a river. The girl in the box is taken by a young man, sometimes a prince, and becomes his wife. A tiger or a lion is then put into the box, and when the teacher, a great way down the river, takes the box and wishes to run away with the girl inside, he is torn to pieces, as a fit reward for his evil intentions, by the beast. But here the story takes a different turn.

own fashion.

As soon as the robbers had left the place Chandralêkhâ came out, and, taking possession of the robbers' rod, took out the eight boxes that the robbers had buried. With these she quickly hastened home, where her mother was awaiting her return. She soon made her appearance, and related all that had occurred during the night to her mother. They soon removed the contents of the boxes and locked them up safely. Then, taking the empty boxes, she filled them up with stones, old iron and other useless materials, and, arranging them two and two by the side of each leg of her cot, went to sleep on it.

As the night was drawing to a close, the robbers, with still more booty, came to the ground, and were thunderstruck when they missed their boxes. But as the day was dawning they went away into the jungle, leaving the investigation of the matter to the next night. They were astonished at the trick that had been played upon them and were very anxious to find out the thief who had outwitted thieves. Now they were sure that their boring-rod, which they had aimed against the unknown person who might be lurking in the *smaśânam* (cremation-ground), must have wounded him. So one of them assumed the guise of an ointment-seller,[96] and, with some ointment in a cocoanut-bottle, began to walk the streets of Kaivalyam city, crying out:—

"Ointment to sell. The best of ointments to cure new wounds and old sores. Please buy my ointment."

And the other seven thieves assumed seven different disguises and also went wandering round the streets of the city. A maid-servant of Chandralêkhâ had seen that her mistress was suffering from the effects of a wound in her back, and never suspecting a thief in the medicine seller, called out to the ointment-man and took him inside the house. She then informed Chandralêkhâ that she had brought in an ointment-man, and that she would do well to buy a little of his medicine for her wound. The clever Chandralêkhâ at once recognised the thief in the medicine vendor, and he too, as he was a very cunning brute, recognised in the young lady the thief of his boxes, and found her wound to be that made by his boring-rod. They soon parted company. The lady bought a little ointment, and the thief in disguise, gladly giving a little of his precious stuff from his cocoanut-bottle, went away. The eight thieves had appointed a place outside Kaivalyam for their rendezvous, and there they learnt who had robbed them of their treasure. Not wishing to remain idle, they chose that very night both to break into Chandralêkhâ's house and bring away herself and their boxes.

Chandralêkhâ, too, was very careful. She locked up all the treasures and kept the eight boxes filled with rubbish, so as to correspond with their original weights, under the cot on which she slept, or rather pretended to sleep, that night. The thieves in due course made a hole into her bedroom and entered. They found her to all appearance sound asleep, and to their still greater joy, they found beneath her cot their eight boxes.

---

[96] From this point up to the end we shall find the story to be similar to "Alî Bâbâ and the Forty Thieves" in the *Arabian Nights,* though the plot is different.

"The vixen is asleep. Let us come to-morrow night and take her away; but first let us remove our boxes."

So saying to each other, they took their boxes, each placing one on his head, and returned in haste to their cave, which they reached early in the morning. But when they opened the boxes to sort out their booty, astonishment of astonishments, their eyes met only broken pieces of stone, lumps of iron, and other such rubbish. Every one of them placed his forefinger at right angles to the tip of his nose, and exclaimed:—

"Ah! A very clever girl. She has managed to deceive us all. But let this day pass. We shall see whether she will not fall into our hands to-night."

Thus, in wonder and amazement, they spent the whole day. Nor was Chandralêkhâ idle at her own house. She was sure she would again see the robbers in her room that night, and, in order to be prepared for the occasion, she made a small sharp knife out of the robber's rod, and kept it beneath her pillow, in the place where she was accustomed to keep her purse containing a few betel leaves, nuts, *chuṇam*, &c., to chew. The night came on. Early Chandralêkhâ had her supper and retired to bed. Sleep she could not, but she cunningly kept eyelids closed and pretended to sleep. Even before it was midnight the eight thieves broke into her room, saying to themselves:—

"This clever lady-thief sleeps soundly. We will do her no mischief here. Let us range ourselves two and two at each leg of her cot, and carry her away unconscious to the woods. There we can kill her."

Thus thinking, the eight thieves ranged themselves at the side of the four legs of the cot, and, without the slightest shaking, removed the cot with the sleeper on it outside the town. Their joy in thus having brought away their enemy was very great, and, not fearing for the safe custody of their prisoner, they marched to their cave. Meanwhile Chandralêkhâ was not idle on the cot. The way to the jungle was through a long and fine avenue of mango trees. It was the mango season, and all the branches were hanging with bunches of ripe and unripe fruit. To make up for her weight on the cot she kept plucking mango bunches and heaping them on it, and as soon as a quantity which she thought would make up her weight was upon her cot, she without the slightest noise took hold of a branch and swung herself off it. The thieves walked on as before, the weight on their heads not apparently diminishing, leaving our heroine safely seated on a mango branch to pass the few remaining *ghaṭikâs* of that anxious night there. The thieves reached their cave just at daybreak, and when they placed their burden down their eyes met only bunches of ripe mangoes, and not the lady they looked for.

"Is she a woman of flesh and blood, or is she a devil?" asked the chief of the next in rank.

"My lord! she is a woman fast enough, and if we search in the wood we shall find her," replied he, and at once all the eight robbers after a light breakfast began to search for her.

Meanwhile the morning dawned upon Chandralêkhâ and let her see that she was in the midst of a thick jungle. She feared to escape in the daytime as the way was long, and she was sure that the robbers would soon be after her. So she resolved to conceal herself in some deep ambush and wait for the night. Before she left the cot for the mango branch she had secured in her hip the small knife she had made for herself out of the robbers' rod and the purse containing the materials for chewing betel; and near the tree into which she had climbed she saw a deep hollow surrounded by impenetrable reeds on all sides. So she slowly let herself down from the tree into this hollow, and anxiously waited there for the night.

All this time the eight thieves were searching for her in different places, and one of them came to the spot where Chandralêkhâ had sat in the tree, and the dense bushes near made him suspect that she was hidden there; so he proceeded to examine the place by climbing up the tree. When Chandralêkhâ saw the thief on the tree she gave up all hopes of life. But suddenly a bright thought came into her mind, just as the man up above saw her. Putting on a most cheerful countenance she slowly spoke to him.

"My dear husband, for I must term you so from this moment, since God has elevated you now to that position, do not raise an alarm. Come down here gently, that we may be happy in each other's company. You are my husband and I am your wife from this moment."

So spoke the clever Chandralêkhâ, and the head of the thief began to turn with joy when he heard so sweet a speech, and forgetting all her previous conduct to himself and his brethren, he leapt into the hollow. She welcomed him with a smiling face, in which the eager heart of the robber read sincere affection, and gave him some betel-nut to chew and chewed some herself merrily. Now redness of the tongue after chewing betel is always an indication of the mutual affection of a husband and wife among the illiterate of Hindu society. So while the betel-leaf was being chewed she put out her tongue to show the thief how red it was, letting him see thereby how deeply she loved him: and he, to show in return how deeply he loved her, put out his tongue too. And she, as if examining it closely, clutched it in her left hand, while with her right hand in the twinkling of an eye cut off the tongue and nose of the robber, and taking advantage of the confusion that came over him she cut his throat and left him dead.

By this time evening was fast approaching, and the other seven robbers, after fruitless search, returned to their cave, feeling sure that the eighth man must have discovered Chandralêkhâ. They waited and waited the whole night, but no one returned, for how could a man who had been killed come back?

Our heroine, meanwhile, as soon as evening set in started homewards, being emboldened by the occasion and the circumstances in which she was placed. She reached home safely at midnight and related all her adventures to her mother. Overcome by exhaustion she slept the rest of the night, and as soon as morning dawned began to strengthen the walls of her bedroom by iron plates. To her most useful pocket-knife she now added a bagful of powdered chillies, and went to bed, not to sleep, but to watch for the robbers. Just as she expected, a small hole was bored in the east wall of her bedroom, and one of the seven robbers thrust in his head. As soon as she saw the hole our heroine stood by the side of it with the powder and knife, and with the latter she cut off the nose of the man who peeped in and thrust the powder into the wound. Unable to bear the burning pain he dragged himself back, uttering *"ṅa, ṅa, ṅa, ṅa,"* having now no nose to pronounce properly with. A second thief, abusing the former for having lost his nose so carelessly, went in, and the bold lady inside dealt in the same way with his nose, and he too, dragged himself back in the same way, calling out *"ṅa, ṅa, ṅa, ṅa."* A third thief abused the second in his turn, and going in lost his nose also. Thus all the seven thieves lost their noses, and, fearing to be discovered if they remained, ran off to the forest, where they had to take a few days' rest from their plundering habits to cure their mutilated noses.

Chandralêkhâ had thus three or four times disappointed the thieves. The more she disappointed them the more she feared for her own safety, especially as she had now inflicted a life-long shame on them.

"The thieves will surely come as soon as their noses are cured and kill me in some way or other. I am, after all, only a girl," she thought to herself. So she went at once to the palace and reported all her adventures with the eight robbers to the prince, who had been her former class-mate. The prince was astonished at the bravery of Chandralêkhâ, and promised the next time the robbers came to lend her his assistance. So every night a spy from the palace slept in Chandralêkhâ's house to carry the news of the arrival of the robbers to the prince, should they ever go there. But the robbers were terribly afraid of approaching Chandralêkhâ's house, after they came to know that she had a knife made out of the boring-rod. But they devised among themselves a plan of inviting Chandralêkhâ to the forest under the pretence of holding a *nautch,* and sent to her house a servant for that purpose. The servant came, and, entering Chandralêkhâ's house, spoke thus to her:—

"My dear young lady, whoever you may be, you have now a chance of enriching yourself. I see plainly from the situation of your house that you are one of the dancing-girls' caste. My masters in the forest have made a plan to give a *nautch* to their relatives on the occasion of a wedding which is to take place there the day after to-morrow. If you come there they will reward you with a *karôṛ* of *mohars* for every *nimisha* (minute) of your performance."

Thus spoke the servant, and Chandralêkhâ, knowing that the mission was from the thieves, agreed to perform the *nautch,* and, asking the man to come and take her and her party the next morning to the forest, sent him away.

In order to lose no time she went at once to the prince and told him all about the *nautch*. Said she:—

"I know very well that this is a scheme of the thieves to kill me, but before they can do that we must try to kill them. A way suggests itself to me in this wise. To make up a *nautch* party more than seven persons are required. One must play the drum; a second must sound the cymbals; a third must blow upon the *nâgasvara* pipe, etc., etc. So I request you to give me seven of your strongest men to accompany me disguised as men of my party, and some of your troops must secretly lie in ambush in readiness to take the robbers prisoners when a signal is given to them."

Thus Chandralêkhâ spoke, and all her advice the prince received with great admiration. He himself offered to follow her as her drummer for the *nautch,* and he chose six of the ablest commanders from his army, and asked them to disguise themselves as fiddlers, pipers, etc., and he directed an army of a thousand men to follow their footsteps at a distance of two *ghaṭikâs'* march, and to lie in ambush near the place where they were going to perform the *nautch,* ready for a call. Thus everything was arranged and all were ready by the morning to start from Chandralêkhâ's house.

Before the third *ghaṭikâ* of the morning was over, the robbers' servant came to conduct Chandralêkhâ with her party to the forest, where the prince and six of his strongest men disguised as her followers, were waiting for him. Chandralêkhâ with all her followers accompanied him, but as soon as she left her house a spy ran off to the army, which, as ordered by the prince, began to follow her party at a distance of two *ghaṭikâs*.

After travelling a long way Chandralêkhâ and her party reached the *nautch* pavilion at about five *ghaṭikâs* before sunset. All their hosts were without their noses, and some still had their noses bandaged up. When they saw that Chandralêkhâ's followers had a fine and prepossessing appearance, even the hard hearts of the robbers softened a little.

"Let us have a look at her performance. She is now entirely in our possession. Instead of murdering her now, we will witness her performance for a *ghaṭikâ,*" said the robbers to each other; and all with one voice said "agreed," and at once the order for the performance was given.

Chandralêkhâ, who was clever in every department of knowledge, began her performance, and, by the most exquisite movement of her limbs, held the audience spell-bound, when suddenly *tâ tai, tôm* clashed the cymbals. This was the signal for the destruction of the robbers, as well as the sign of the close of a part of the *nautch.* In the twinkling of an eye the seven disguised followers of the dancing-girl had thrown down the thieves and were upon them. Before the servants of the robbers could come to the help of their masters the footsteps of an army near were heard, and in no time the prince's one thousand men were on the spot and took all the robbers and their followers prisoners.

So great had been the ravages of these robbers in and round Kaivalyam that, without any mercy being shown to them, they and their followers were all ordered to be beheaded, and the prince was so much won over by the excellent qualities of Chandralêkhâ that, notwithstanding her birth as a dancing-girl, he regarded her as a gem of womankind and married her.

"Buy a girl in a *bâzâr*" (*kanniyai kaḍaiyir koḷ*) is a proverb. What matter where a girl is born provided she is virtuous! And Chandralêkhâ, by her excellent virtue, won a prince for her lord. And when that lord came to know of the real nature of his teacher, who was also the teacher of Chandralêkhâ, he banished him from his kingdom, as a merciful punishment, in consideration of his previous services.

## CHAPTER XIX.

### THE CONQUEST OF FATE.

In the Dakshinadêśa there lived a Brâhmiṇ boy who from his childhood was given a very liberal education in Sanskṛit. He had read so much in philosophy that before he reached the sixteenth year of his life he began to despise the pleasures of the world. Everything which he saw was an illusion (*mithyâ*) to him. So he resolved to renounce the world and to go to a forest, there to meet with some great sage, and pass his days with him in peace and happiness.

Having thus made up his mind, he left his home one day without the knowledge of his parents and travelled towards the Dandakâranya. After wandering for a long time in that impenetrable forest, and undergoing all the miseries of a wood inhabited only by wild beasts, he reached the banks of the Tuṅgabhadrâ. His sufferings in his wanderings in a forest untrodden by human feet, his loneliness in the midst of wild beasts, his fears whether after all he had not failed in his search for consolation in a preceptor to teach him the higher branches of philosophy, came up one after another before his mind. Dejected and weary, he cast his glance forward as far as it could reach. Was it a reality or only imagination? He saw before him a lonely cottage of leaves (*parṇaśâlâ*). To a lonely traveller even the appearance of shelter is welcome, so he followed up his vision till it became a reality, and an aged hoary Brâhmiṇ, full fourscore and more in years, welcomed our young philosopher.

"What has brought you here, my child, to this lonely forest thus alone?" spoke in a sweet voice the hoary lord of the cottage of leaves.

"A thirst for knowledge, so that I may acquire the mastery over the higher branches of philosophy," was the reply of our young adventurer, whose name was Subrahmanya.

"Sit down my child," said the old sage, much pleased that in this Kaliyuga, which is one long epoch of sin, there was at least one young lad who had forsaken his home for philosophy.

Having thus seen our hero safely relieved from falling a prey to the tigers and lions of the Dandakâranya, let us enquire into the story of the old sage. In the good old days even of this Kaliyuga learned people, after fully enjoying the world, retired to the forests, with or without their wives, to pass the decline of life in solemn solitude and contemplation. When they went with their wives they were said to undergo the *vânaprastha* stage of family life.

The hoary sage of our story was undergoing *vânaprastha,* for he was in the woods with his wife. His name while living was Jñânanidhi. He had built a neat *parṇaśâlâ,* or cottage of leaves, on the banks of the commingled waters of the Tuṅgâ and Bhadrâ, and here his days and nights were spent in meditation. Though old in years he retained the full vigour of manhood, the result of a well-spent youth. The life of his later years was most simple and sinless.

"Remote from man, with God he passed his days;
Prayer all his business, all his pleasures praise."

The wood yielded him herbs, fruits, and roots, and the river, proverbial[97] for its sweet waters, supplied him with drink. He lived, in fact, as simply as the bard who sang:—

"But from the mountain's grassy side
A guiltless feast I bring;
A bag with herbs and fruits supplied,
And water from the spring."

His faithful wife brought him these, while Jñânanidhi himself devoted his whole time to the contemplation of God.

Such was Jñânanidhi—the abode of all wise people—to whom the boy-philosopher, Subrahmanya, resorted. After questioning each other both were mightily pleased at the fortune which had brought them together. Jñânanidhi was glad to impart his hard-earned knowledge during his leisure moments to the young student, and Subrahmanya, with that longing which made him renounce the city and take to the woods eagerly swallowed and assimilated whatever was administered to him. He relieved his mother—for as such he regarded his master's wife—of all her troubles, and used, himself, to go out to bring the fruits, herbs, and roots necessary for the repasts of the little family. Thus passed five years, by which time our young friend had become learned in the many branches of Aryan philosophy.

Jñânanidhi had a desire to visit the source of the Tuṅgabhadrâ, but his wife was eight months advanced in her pregnancy. So he could not take her; and to take care of her he had to leave behind his disciple, Subrahmanya. Thus after commending the lady to Subrahmanya's care, and leaving for female assistance another sage's wife, whom he had brought from a distant forest, Jñânanidhi went his way.

Now, there is a strong belief among Hindus that Brahmâ, the great creator, writes on everyone's head at the time of his birth his future fortunes in life. He is supposed to do this just at the moment of birth. Of course, the great god when he enters the room to discharge his onerous duty, is invisible to all human eyes. But the eyes of Subrahmanya were not exactly human. The supreme knowledge which Jñânanidhi had imparted to him made it easy for him to discern at once a person entering most impolitely the room in which his master's wife had been confined.

"Let your reverence stop here," said the disciple angrily though respectfully.

The great god shuddered, for he had been in the habit of entering hourly innu-

[97] *Gaṅgâ snâna Tuṅga pâna.* The Ganges for bath and Tuṅga (Tuṅgabhadrâ) for drink.

merable buildings on his eternal rounds of duty, but never till then had a human being perceived him and asked him to stop. His wonder knew no measure, and as he stood bewildered the following reprimand fell on his ears:

"Hoary Brâhmiṇ sage (for so Brahmâ appeared), it is unbecoming your age thus to enter the hut of my master, unallowed by me, who am watching here. My teacher's wife is ill. Stop!"

Brahmâ hastily—for the time of inscribing the future fortune on the forehead of the baby to be born was fast approaching—explained to Subrahmanya who he was and what had brought him there. As soon as our young hero came to know the person who stood before him he rose up, and, tying his upper cloth round his hips as a mark of respect, went round the creator thrice, fell down before Brahmâ's most holy feet and begged his pardon. Brahmâ had not much time. He wanted to go in at once, but our young friend would not leave the god until he explained what he meant to write on the head of the child.

"My son!" said Brahmâ, "I myself do not know what my iron nail will write on the head of the child. When the child is born I place the nail on its head, and the instrument writes the fate of the baby in proportion to its good or bad acts in its former life. To delay me is merely wrong. Let me go in."

"Then," said Subrahmanya, "your holiness must inform me when your holiness goes out what has been written on the child's head."

"Agreed," said Brahmâ and went in. After a moment he returned, and our young hero at the door asked the god what his nail had written.

"My child!" said Brahmâ, "I will inform you what it wrote; but if you disclose it to anyone your head will split into a thousand pieces. The child is a male child. It has before it a very hard life. A buffalo and a sack of grain will be its livelihood. What is to be done. Perhaps it had not done any good acts in its former life, and as the result of its sin it must undergo miseries now."

"What! Your supreme holiness, the father of this child is a great sage! And is this the fate reserved to the son of a sage?" wept the true disciple of the sage.

"What have I to do with the matter? The fruits of acts in a former life must be undergone in the present life. But, remember, if you should reveal this news to any one your head will split into a thousand pieces."

Having said this Brahmâ went away, leaving Subrahmanya extremely pained to hear that the son of a great sage was to have a hard life. He could not even open his lips on the subject, for if he did his head would be split. In sorrow he passed some days, when Jñânanidhi returned from his pilgrimage and was delighted to see his wife and the child doing well, and in the learned company of the old sage our young disciple forgot all his sorrow.

Three more years passed away in deep study, and again the old sage wanted to go on a pilgrimage to the sacred source of the Tuṅgabhadrâ. Again was his wife expecting her confinement, and he had to leave her and his disciple behind with the usual temporary female assistance. Again, too, did Brahmâ come at the moment of birth, but found easy admittance as Subrahmanya had now become acquainted with him owing to the previous event. Again did Brahmâ take an oath from him not to communicate the fortunes of the second child, with the curse that if he broke his oath, his head would split into a thousand pieces. This child was a female, and the nail had written that her fate was to be that of a frivolous woman. Extremely vexed was our young philosopher. The thought vexed him to such a degree, that language has no words to express it. After worrying a great deal he consoled himself with the soothing philosophies of the fatalists, that fate alone governs the world.

The old sage in due course returned, and our young disciple spent two more happy years with him. After a little more than ten years had been thus spent the boy reached to five years and the girl to two. The more they advanced in years the more did the recollection of their future pain Subrahmanya. So one morning he humbly requested the old sage to permit him to go on a long journey to the Himâlayas and other mountains, and Jñânanidhi, knowing that all that he knew had been grasped by the young disciple, permitted him with a glad heart to satisfy his curiosity.

Our hero started, and after several years, during which he visited several towns and learned men, reached the Himâlayas. There he saw many sages, and lived with them for some time. He did not remain in one place, for his object was more to examine the world. So he went from place to place, and after a long and interesting journey of twenty years he again returned to the banks of the Tuṅgabhadrâ, at the very place where he lived for ten years and imbibed philosophical knowledge from Jñânanidhi. But he saw there neither Jñânanidhi nor his old wife. They had long since fallen a prey to the lord of death. Much afflicted at heart at seeing his master and mistress no more, he went to the nearest town, and there after a deal of search he found a coolie with a single buffalo. The fate which Brahmâ's nail had written on his master's son rushed into the mind of Subrahmanya. He approached the coolie, and, on closely examining him from a distance, our hero found distinct indications of his master's face in the labourer. His grief knew no bounds at seeing the son of a great sage thus earning his livelihood by minding a buffalo. He followed him to his home, and found that he had a wife and two children. One sack of corn he had in his house and no more, from which he took out a portion every day and gave it to his wife to be shelled. The rice was cooked, and with the petty earnings of a coolie, he and his family kept body and soul together. Each time the corn in the sack became exhausted he used to be able to save enough to replenish it again with corn. Thus did he (according to the writing of Brahmâ's nail) pass his days. Kapâlî was the name of this coolie, the sage's son.

"Do you know me, Kapâlî?" said our hero, as he remembered his name.

The coolie was astonished to hear his name so readily pronounced by one who was apparently a stranger to him, but he said:—

"I am sorry that I do not know you, Sir."

Subrahmanya then explained to him who he was, and requested him to follow his advice.

"My dear son," said he, "do as I bid you. Early morning to-morrow leave your bed and take to the market your buffalo and the corn sack. Dispose of them for whatever amount they will fetch. Do not think twice about the matter. Buy all that is necessary for a sumptuous meal from the sale proceeds and eat it all up at once without reserving a morsel for the morrow. You will get a great deal more than you can eat in a day; but do not reserve any, even the smallest portion of it. Feed several other Brâhmiṇs with it. Do not think that I advise you for your ruin. You will see in the end that what your father's disciple tells you is for your own prosperity."

However, whatever the sage might say, Kapâlî could not bring himself to believe him.

"What shall I do to feed my wife and children to-morrow if I sell everything belonging to me to-day?"

Thus thought Kapâlî, and consulted his wife.

Now she was a very virtuous and intelligent woman. Said she:—

"My dear lord, we have heard that your father was a great *mahâtmâ.* This disciple must equally be a *mahâtmâ.* His holiness would not advise us to our ruin. Let us follow the sage's advice."

When Kapâlî's wife thus supported the sage, he resolved to dispose of his beast and sack the next morning, and he did so accordingly. The provisions he bought were enough to feed fifty Brâhmiṇs morning and evening, as well as his own family. So that day he fed Brâhmiṇs for the first time in his life. Night came on, and after an adventurous day Kapâlî retired to sleep, but sleep he could not. Meanwhile Subrahmanya was sleeping on the bare verandah outside the house, and he came to the sage and said:—

"Holy sage, nearly half the night is spent, and there are only fifteen *ghaṭikâs* more for the dawn. What shall I do for the morrow for my hungry children? All that I had I have spent. I have not even a morsel of cold rice for the morning."

Subrahmanya showed him some money that he had in his hand, enough to buy a buffalo and a sack of corn in case the great god did not help him, and asked him to spend that night, at least the remainder of it, in calm sleep. So Kapâlî, with his heart at ease, retired to rest.

He had not slept more than ten *ghaṭikâs* when he dreamt that all his family—his wife and children—were screaming for a mouthful of rice. Suddenly he awoke and cursed his poverty which always made such thoughts dwell uppermost in his mind. There were only five *ghaṭikâs* for the lord of the day to make his appearance in the eastern horizon, and before this could happen he wanted to finish his morning bath and ablutions, and so he went to his garden to bathe at the well. The shed for the buffalo was erected in the garden, and it had been his habit daily before bathing to give fresh straw to his beast. That morning he thought he would be spared that duty. But, wonder of wonders! He saw another buffalo standing there. He cursed his poverty again which made him imagine impossibilities. How could it be possible that his beast should be standing there when he had sold it the previous morning? So he went into the shed and found a real buffalo standing there. He could not believe his eyes, and hastily brought a lamp from his house. It was, however, a real buffalo, and beside it was a sack of corn! His heart leapt with joy, and he ran out to tell his patron, Subrahmanya. But when the latter heard it he said with a disgusted air:—

"My dear Kapâlî, why do you care so much? Why do you feel so overjoyed? Take the beast at once with the corn-sack and sell them as you did yesterday."

Kapâlî at once obeyed the orders and changed the money into provisions. Again fifty Brâhmiṇs were fed the next day too, and nothing was reserved for the third day's use. Thus it went on in Kapâlî's house. Every morning he found a buffalo and a sack of corn, which he sold and fed Brâhmiṇs with the proceeds. In this way a month passed. Said Subrahmanya one day:—

"My dear Kapâlî, I am your holy father's disciple, and I would never advise you to do a thing prejudicial to your welfare. When I came to know that you were the son of the great sage, Jñânanidhi, and were leading so wretched a life, I came to see you in order to alleviate your miseries. I have now done so, having pointed out the way to you to live comfortably. Daily must you continue thus. Do as you have been doing for the past month, and never store away anything, for if you reserve a portion all this happiness may fail, and you will have to revert to your former wretched life. I have done my duty towards you. If you become ambitious of hoarding up money this good fortune may desert you."

Kapâlî agreed to follow the advice of the sage to the uttermost detail and requested him to remain in his house. Again said Subrahmanya:—

"My son! I have better work before me than living in your house. So please excuse me. But before leaving you, I request you to inform me as to where your sister is. She was a child of two years of age when I saw her twenty years ago. She must be about twenty-two or twenty-three now. Where is she?"

Tears trickled down the eyes of Kapâlî when his sister was mentioned. Said he:—

"Do not, my patron, think of her. She is lost to the world. I am ashamed to think of her. Why should we think of such a wretch at this happy time?"

At once the inscription made by Brahmâ's nail rushed into Subrahmanya's mind and he understood what was meant. Said he:—

"Never mind; be open and tell me where she is."

Then her brother, Kapâlî, with his eyes still wet with tears, said that his sister, the daughter of the sage Jñânanidhi, was leading the worst of lives in an adjoining village, and that her name was Kalyânî.

Subrahmanya took leave of Kapâlî and his wife, after blessing his little children and again warning his friend. He had conferred what happiness he could upon his master's son, and now the thought of reforming his master's daughter reigned supreme in his heart. He went at once to the village indicated and reached it at about nightfall. After an easy search he found her house and knocked at the door. The door was at once opened. But on that day she was astonished to see a face such as she could never expect to approach her house.

"Do you know me, Kalyânî?" said Subrahmanya, and she in reply said that she did not. He then explained who he was, and when she came to know that it was a disciple of her father that was standing before her she wept most bitterly. The thought that after having been born of such a holy sage, she had adopted so wretched a life, the most shameful in the world, made her miserable at heart. She fell down at his feet and asked to be forgiven. She then explained to him her extreme misery, and the hard necessity which had compelled her to take to her present way of living. He then consoled her and spoke thus:—

"My dear daughter! My heart burns within me when I see that necessity has driven you to this wretched life. But I can redeem you if you will only follow my advice. From this night you had better shut your door, and never open it to any other person except to him who brings to you a large measure full of pearls of the first water. You follow this advice for a day and I shall then advise you further."

Being the daughter of a great sage, and having been compelled by necessity to take to a wretched life, she readily consented to follow her father's disciple when he promised to redeem her. She bolted the door, and refused admission to anyone unless they brought a large measure full of pearls. Her visitors, fancying that she must have gone mad, went away. The night was almost drawing to a close and all her friends had gone away disappointed. Who was there in the village to give to her one measure full of pearls? But as the nail of Brahmâ had appointed for her such a life as stated, some one was bound to comply with her terms. And as there was no human being who could do so, the god Brahmâ himself assumed the shape of a young man, and, with a measure full of pearls, visited her in the last watch of the night and remained with her.

When morning dawned he disappeared, and when Kalyânî explained to the disciple of her father the next morning that after all one person had visited her with a measure full of pearls on the previous night, he was glad to hear of it. He knew that his plan was working well. Said he:—

"My dear daughter, you are restored to your former good self hereafter from this day. There are very few people in this world who could afford to give you a measure full of pearls every night. So he that brought you the pearls last night must continue to do so every night, and he shall be hereafter your only husband. No other person must ever hereafter see your face, and you must obey my orders. You must sell all the pearls he brings you every day and convert them into money. This money you should spend in feeding the poor and other charities. None of it must you reserve for the next day, neither must you entertain a desire to hoard up money. The day you fail to follow my advice you will lose your husband, and then you will have to fall back on your former wretched life."

Thus said Subrahmanya, and Kalyânî agreed to strictly follow his injunctions. He then went to live under a tree opposite to her house for a month to see whether his plan was working well, and found it worked admirably.

Thus, after having conferred happiness, to the best of his abilities, on the son and daughter of his former master, Subrahmanya took leave of Kalyânî, and with her permission, most reluctantly given, he pursued his pilgrimage.

One moonlight night, after a long sleep, Subrahmanya rose up almost at midnight, and hearing the crows crowing he mistook it for the dawn and commenced his journey. He had not proceeded far, when on his way he met a beautiful person coming towards him, with a sack of corn on his head and a bundle of pearls tied up in the end of his upper cloth on his shoulder, leading a buffalo before him.

"Who are you, sir, walking thus in this forest?" said Subrahmanya.

When thus addressed, the person before him threw down the sack and wept most bitterly.

"See, sir, my head is almost become bald by having to bear to Kapâlî's house a sack of corn every night. This buffalo I lead to Kapâlî's shed and this bundle of pearls I take to Kalyânî's house. My nail wrote their fate on their respective heads and by your device I have to supply them with what my nail wrote. When will you relieve me of these troubles?"

Thus wept Brahmâ, for it was no other personage. He was the creator and protector of all beings, and when Subrahmanya had pointed out the way for his master's children, and they had conquered fate, Brahmâ too was conquered. So the great god soon gave them eternal felicity and relieved himself of his troubles.

# CHAPTER XX.

## THE BRÂHMAṆ PRIEST WHO BECAME AN AMILDÂR.[98]

In the Karnâta dêśa there reigned a famous king named Châmunḍa, who was served by an household priest, named Gunḍappa, well versed in all the rituals at which he officiated.

Châmunḍa, one day, while chewing betel-leaves, thus addressed Gunḍappa, who was sitting opposite him:—

"My most holy priest, I am greatly pleased at your faithfulness in the discharge of your sacred duties; and you may ask of me now what you wish and I shall grant your request."

The priest elated replied: "I have always had a desire to become the *Amildâr*[99] of a district and to exercise power over a number of people; and if your Majesty should grant me this I shall have attained my ambition."

"Agreed," said the king, and at that time the *Amildârship* of Nañjaṅgôḍ happening to be vacant, his Majesty at once appointed his priest to the post, thinking that his priest, who was intelligent in his duties, would do well in the new post. Before he sent him off, however, he gave Gunḍappa three bits of advice:—

(1). *Mukha kappage irabêku.*

(2). *Ellâru kevianna kachchi mâtan âḍu.*

(3). *ellâr juṭṭu kayyalii irabêku.*

The meaning of which is:

(1). You should always keep a black (*i.e.* frowning) countenance.

(2). When you speak about State affairs you should do it biting the ear (*i.e.* secretly—close to the ear).

(3.) The locks of every one should be in your hand (*i.e.* you must use your influence and make every one subservient to you).

Gunḍappa heard these words so kindly given by the king, and the way in which he listened to them made his Majesty understand that he had taken them to heart. So with a smiling face the king gave the letter containing the appointment to Gunḍappa, who returned home with an elated heart.

[98] A Kanarese tale related by a risâldâr.

[99] Headman of the village.

He told his wife about the change that had come over his prospects, and wished to start at once to take charge of the new post. The king and his officers at once sent messengers to Nañjaṅgôḍ informing the officers of the *Amîldârî* that a newly appointed *Amîldâr* would be coming soon. So they all waited near the gate of the town to pay their respects to the new *Amîldâr* and escort him into it.

Gunḍappa started the very next morning to Nañjaṅgôḍ with a bundle containing clean clothes, six by twelve cubits long, on his head. Poor priest! Wherever he saw the *kuśa* grass on the road, he was drawn to it by its freshness, and kept on storing it up all the way. The sacred grass had become so dear to him, that, though he would have no occasion to use it as *Amîldâr* of Nañjaṅgôḍ, he could not pass by it without gathering some of it. So with his bundle of clothes on his head and his beloved *kuśa* grass in his hands, Gunḍappa approached the city of Nañjaṅgôḍ about the twentieth *ghaṭikâ* of the day.

Now, though it was very late in the day, none of the officers, who had come out to receive the *Amildâr* had returned home to their meals. Everyone was waiting in the gate and when Gunḍappa turned up, no one took him to be anything more than a priest. The bundle on his head and the green ritual grass in his hands proclaimed his vocation. But everyone thought that, as a priest was coming by the very road the *Amildâr* would take, he might bring news of him—whether he had halted on the road and would or might be expected before the evening. So the next officer in rank to the *Amildâr* came to the most reverend priest and asked him whether he had any news of the coming *Amildâr*; on which our hero put down his bundle and taking out the cover containing the order of his appointment with a handful of *kuśa* grass, lest his clothes be polluted if he touched them with his bare hands informed his subordinate that he was himself the *Amildâr*!

All those assembled were astonished to find such a wretched priest appointed to so responsible a post, but when it was made known that Gunḍappa was the new *Amildâr* the customary music was played and he was escorted in a manner due to his position, into the town. He had been fasting from the morning, and a grand feast was prepared for him in the house of the next senior official, which Gunḍappa entered for a dinner and rest. He there informed the officials that he would be at the office at the twenty-fifth *ghaṭikâ* of the evening. From the way in which he issued the order all thought that he was really an able man, and that he had come in the guise of a simple priest in order to find out the real state of his district. So every officer went home, bathed, had his meal in haste and attended at the office.

The chief assistant took the *Amildâr* to his house, and entertained his guest as became his position. Gunḍappa, being a priest, was a very good eater, for never for a day in his life had he spent money out of his own pocket on meals, so what reason had he to enquire about the price of provisions? It was at the expense of others he had grown so fat! And doing more than full justice to all the good things, much to the secret amusement of his host and assistant, Gunḍappa rose up from his food, and washed his hands. He then wanted betel-leaves though to ask for these before the host offers them is very impolite. But his subordinate interpreted it as an order from a master and brought the platter containing the necessary nutmeg, mace, nut, leaves, and *chuṇam* (lime).

"Where is the dakshiṇa?"[100] next asked the *Amildâr*. His host did not quite understand whether this was meant in earnest or in joke, but before he could solve the question in his mind:—

"Where is the *dakshiṇâ*?" reiterated the *Amildâr*, and his assistant, thinking that his new superior was prone to taking bribes, at once brought a bag containing 500 *mohars* and placed it in the platter. Now a *dakshiṇa* to a Brâhmiṇ is not usually more than a couple of rupees, but should an *Amildâr* ask for one, his assistant would naturally mistake him, and think he was hinting at a bribe!

Gunḍappa greatly pleased at a princely *dakshiṇa* such as he had never seen before in all his life, at once opened the bag and counted out every gold piece in it, carefully tying them up in his bundle. He then began to chew his betel, and at one gulp swallowed up all the nutmeg and mace in the platter! All this made his assistant strongly suspect the real nature of the new *Amildâr*; but then there was the order of the king, and it must be obeyed! Gunḍappa next asked his assistant to go on in advance of him to the office, saying that he would be there himself in a *ghaṭikâ*. The assistant accordingly left a messenger to attend on the *Amildâr*, and being very anxious to see things in good order, left his house for the office.

Gunḍappa now remembered the three bits of advice given by the king, the first of which was that he should always put on, when in office, a black countenance. Now he understood the word "black" in its literal sense, and not in its allegorical one of "frowning," and, so going into the kitchen, he asked for a lump of charcoal paste. When this was ready he blackened the whole of his face with it, and covering his face with his cloth—as he was ashamed to show it—entered the office. With his face thus blackened and partly covered with a cloth, the new *Amildâr* came and took his seat. Now and then he would remove the cloth from his eyes to see how his officers were working, and meanwhile all the clerks and others present were laughing in their sleeves at the queer conduct of their chief.

The evening was drawing to a close, and there were certain orders to be signed: so taking them all in his hand the assistant approached the *Amildâr*, and stood at a respectful distance. Gunḍappa, however, asked him to come nearer, and nearer the assistant came.

"Still nearer," said Gunḍappa, and nearer still came the assistant.

The second bit of advice from the king now rushed into the *Amildâr's* mind that he should bite the ears of his officials when he enquired into State affairs, and as Gunḍappa's want of sense always made him take what was said literally, he opened his mouth and bit the ear of his assistant, while in a muffled voice he asked him whether all his people enjoyed full prosperity! The assistant, now in very fear of his life, roared out that all the people were enjoying the greatest prosperity. But Gunḍappa would not let go his ear till the poor assistant had roared out the answer more than twenty times. The poor wretch's ear soon began to swell enormously, and leaving the office in disgust, he started to report to the king the insane acts of the new *Amildâr*.

Two out of the three bits of advice from the king had now been duly obeyed,

[100] *Dakshiṇâs* (fees given in donation to Brâhmiṇs) are ordinarily given to priests.

but the third, that the locks of all the people must be in his hands, remained unfulfilled, and Gunḍappa wished to carry out that also quickly. Night had now set in, and as the *Amildâr* still remained in his seat, all his officers were compelled to do the same. In this way the tenth *ghaṭikâ* of the night approached, and still the *Amildâr* would not get up, but sat with his black face secured in his cloth, now and then peeping out to see whether they were all asleep or awake. The fact was, he was waiting for an opportunity to have all the locks of his officers in his hand! As soon as all his officers fell asleep he intended to cut off all their locks, as usual understanding the words in their literal sense! At about midnight, never dreaming of the stupid act that the *Amildâr* was contemplating in his mind, every one fell asleep, and Gunḍappa rose up, and with a pair of scissors cut off all the locks of his officers. He then tied them all up in a bundle and returned to his assistant's home late at night, where the servants gave him something to eat; after which he started with his bag of *mohars* and bundle of locks to his king to inform him of how well he had obeyed his orders!

In the early morning he reached the presence of his Majesty only a nimisha after his assistant had arrived. Seeing the *Amildâr* he was too afraid to to lodge any complaint, but his swollen ear drew the attention of every eye in the assembly.

Gunḍappa now stood before the king with the charcoal on his face and said:—

"Most noble king, you ordered me to blacken my face for my new duty. See, I have not even yet removed the dye! You ordered me next only to speak while biting an ear. Look, please, at my assistant's ear, who stands before you and tell me whether I have not obeyed you!! And as for having the locks of my officers in my hands; why here they are in this bundle!!!"

Never had the king seen a similar instance of such stupidity, and the thought that Gunḍappa had shorn so many respectable heads of their locks, and had really bitten the ear of a worthy gentleman, brought much shame to his heart. He begged pardon of the injured man and from that day forward was very careful in the choice of his officers! Poor Gunḍappa was dismissed even from the priestship, and his belly grew lean from having no longer the privilege of eating rich food at others' cost!

# CHAPTER XXI.

## THE GARDENER'S CUNNING WIFE.

In a certain village there lived with his wife a poor gardener who cultivated greens in a small patch in the backyard of his house. They were in thirty little beds, half of which he would water every day. This occupied him from the fifth to the fifteenth *ghaṭikâ*.

His wife used to cut a basketful of greens every evening, and he took them in the mornings to sell in the village. The sale brought him a measure or two of rice, and on this the family lived! If he could manage any extra work of an evening he got a few coppers which served to meet their other expenses.

Now in that village there was a temple to Kâlî, before which was a fine tank with a mango tree on its bank. The fish in the tank and the mangoes from the tree were dedicated to the goddess, and were strictly forbidden to the villagers. If any one was discovered cutting a mango or catching a fish, he was at once excommunicated from the village. So strict was the prohibition.

The gardener was returning home one morning after selling his greens and passed the temple. The mangoes, so carefully guarded by religious protection, were hanging on the tree in great numbers, and the gardener's eyes fell on them! His mouth watered. He looked round about him, and fortunately there was no one by, at least, as far as his eyes could reach. So he hastily plucked one of the mangoes and with nimble feet descended into the tank to wash it. Just then a most charming shoal of fish met his eyes. These protected dwellers in the tank had no notion of danger, and so were frolicking about at their ease. The gardener looked about him first and finding no one by caught half a dozen stout fish at one plunge of his hand. He hid them and the mango underneath the rice in his basket and returned home, happy in the thought that he had not been caught. Now he had a special delight in fish, and when he reached his house he showed what he brought to his wife and asked her to prepare a dish with the newly caught fish and the never-till-then tasted mango.

Meanwhile he had to water his garden, and went to the backyard for the purpose. The watering was done by a *pikôṭa*. He used to run up and down the pole while a friend of his, the son of his neighbour, lifted the water and irrigated the garden.

Meanwhile his wife cooked the dish of mango and fish in a pan, and found the flavour so sweet that even while the fish was only half cooked she began to taste one bit of it after another till more than half had already gone down her throat!

The dish was at last cooked, and the few remaining slices in the pan were taken off the fire, so she went into the verandah and from thence saw her husband running up and down the *pikôṭa*. She beckoned to him that the dish was ready and that he should come in and taste it. However, he never noticed her, but kept on running up and down the *pikôṭa,* and while running up and down he was obliged to wave his hands about, and this his wife mistook as an indication that she might eat up her portion of the dish. At any rate her imagination made her think so; and she went in and ate a slice, and then went out into the verandah again to call her husband who was still running up and down the *pikôṭa*. Again, her husband, so she thought, waved his hands in permission to go on with her dinner. Again she went in and had another slice. Thus it went on for a full *ghaṭikâ* till the last slice was consumed.

"Alas!" thought she, "With what great eagerness my husband fetched the fish and the mango, and how sadly, out of greediness, have I disappointed him. Surely his anger will know no bounds when he comes in. I must soon devise some means to save myself."

So she brought the pan in which she cooked the fish and mango out of the house and covered it with another pan of similar size and sat down before it. Then she undid her hair and twisted it about her head until it was dishevelled. She then began to make a great noise. This action by a woman in an illiterate family of low caste is always supposed to indicate a visitation from a goddess and a demon; so when her husband from the *pikôṭa* tree saw the state of his wife, his guilty conscience smote him. The change in his wife alarmed him, and he came down suddenly and stood before her. As soon as she saw him she roared out at him:—

"Why have you injured me to-day by plundering my mango and fish? How dare you do such an irreligious act? You shall soon see the results of your impertinence!"

"The goddess has come upon my wife most terribly," thought the poor man. "Her divine power may soon kill her! What shall I do?"

So he fell at the feet of the divine visitation as he thought it to be, and said:—

"My most holy goddess, your dog of a servant has this day deviated from the straight path. Excuse him this time, and he will never do so a second time."

"Run then with the pan which contains the fruits of your robbery and dip it deep into my tank. Then shall the fish become alive and the mango shall take its place in the tree."

The gardener received the order most submissively, and taking the pan in his hand flew to the tank. There he dipped it in the water and came back to his house fully believing that his sin that day had been forgiven, and that the cooked fish had become alive again and the mango a living one. Thus did the cunning wife save herself from her husband's wrath!

# CHAPTER XXII.

## KEEP IT FOR THE BEGGAR.

When anything sweet is prepared in the house on a particular night, and when the children, after feeding to their fill, say to the mother:—

"Ammâ, this pudding is sweet; keep it for the morning," the mother says at once:—

"Ask me to keep it for the beggar, and I shall do it."

"Why should I not say keep it for the morning, Ammâ," ask the curious children, and the South Indian mother gives to her listening children the following story:—

In a certain village there lived an affectionate husband and wife. The husband would go to look after the fields and garden and return home with abundance of vegetables. The wife would cook and serve her lord to his fill. Before going out in the morning the husband used to take whatever of last night's dishes were left cold to remain for his breakfast.

The husband was a great eater of *dhâl*[101] soup. Every night the wife used to prepare a large quantity of it and leave a good portion of it to stand for the morning's breakfast of her lord. And he, too, owing to his taste for the cold rice, used to warn his wife—though she was very careful—and say:—

"Keep me some of this soup for the next morning."

The wife used to say: "Yes, my dear husband, I shall do so."

This went on for several years. Every day the *dhâl* soup was invariably prepared for the night meal and a good portion of it was reserved for the cold rice. Every night, the husband, without forgetting for even a single day, used to ask his wife to reserve a portion. Thus passed on several years, as we have already said.

One night this husband had his supper. The wife had sat at her husband's leaf to take her supper after her lord had had his. That night, too, our hero, as usual, repeated:—

"Keep, my dear, some of this soup for the morning."

At once a gurgling laughter was heard near the doorsill of their house. The pair were astonished, and searched their whole house. No one was discovered. Again the husband said:—

[101] A yellow grain, peculiar to India.

"Keep, my dear, some of this soup for the morning."

Again the laughter was heard. Finding that the laughter immediately followed his order, the husband repeated it a third time. A third time also the laughter broke out. They were astonished. Three times had laughter been heard in their house, and still they could see no one. Thinking that some one must have mocked him from the neighbouring houses, he made careful inquiries and satisfied himself that none of his neighbours had mocked him. He was afraid at the laughter which thrice proceeded from a part of his house, as he had heard it distinctly.

That very night our hero had a sudden and unforeseen calamity, and just as he was dragging the latch of his backyard door a serpent stung him in his finger. Neighbours hearing of the venomous reptile in their next house, ran there with a stout cudgel. Already the master of the house, who was passionately fond of the *dhâl* soup, had swooned away. His wife was mourning by his side, saying:—

"My dear husband. How did you forget your soup so soon and leave us all for the other world? Just now you gave me the order, and before tasting it even you have died."

The neighbours began to search for the snake; but they did not succeed. And again a voice exclaimed from vacuum:—

"This husband's fate ended at the twelfth *ghaṭikâ* of this night. Yama ordered me to go and fetch him to his world. I came down and reached this house at the eighth *ghaṭikâ* when the husband was giving the order to reserve for the morning meal his dear *dhâl* soup. I could not contain my laughter, and so broke out with a gurgling noise. As I am divine no one could perceive me. And so none ever found me in this house after they heard the laughter. Then I transformed myself into a serpent and waited for the hour to do my death-dealing duty. The poor man is now no more. Four *ghaṭikâs* ago he was of opinion that he would live and eat his cold rice to-morrow morning. How very sanguine people are in this world of uncertainty. The cause for my laughter was the husband's certainty when he issued that order to reserve the *dhâl* soup for the breakfast."

Thus ended the messenger, and vanished of course to inform his master how he had executed his orders.

And from that day, my children, it was fixed that our life in this world is always uncertain, and that one who lives at this moment cannot be sure of doing so at the next moment. While such is the case, how can you say, "Keep the pudding for to-morrow morning." Since you saw in the story just related to you, that we can never be certain of our life, you must say, instead of "for to-morrow morning, for the beggar." If we keep it for the beggar, and if we fortunately live till to-morrow morning, we shall use a portion of it and give the remainder to the beggar. Hence you must always, hereafter, say when any supper from overnight is to be left for the morning, "Keep it for the beggar, Ammâ."

"Yes, mother. We shall do so hereafter," replied the children.

In India, among Brâhmiṇs, the wife must never take her food before her lord, unless she is pregnant or sick. In these two cases even on the days when it is possible to avoid the meal before her lord, the wife invariably does it; on other days she cannot probably help it when she is physically unable. And in taking her meal, the wife sits in front of the leaf (dish) from which her husband has eaten. Most husbands generally leave their leaves clean, some out of pure affection to their wives and out of a good intention of not injuring the feelings of their wives. But there are others, who, as they are unclean in their other habits, are also unclean in their eating. The appearance of their leaves after they have left off eating, is like those thrown out in the streets and mutilated by crows and dogs. But their wives, cursing their lot to have married such husbands, must, as long as they are orthodox, eat out of those leaves.

# CHAPTER XXIII.

## GOOD LUCK TO THE LUCKY ONE; OR, SHALL I FALL DOWN?

In a certain town there lived a wealthy Brâhmiṇ. He wished to build a house—pretty large and spacious—as became his riches. For that purpose he called in a great number of soothsayers, and fixed, guided by their scientific opinion, a place for building the mansion. A certain portion of every day is supposed to be bad for doing work. This portion is sometimes called the *Râhu-kâḷa*—the evil time of the demon *râhu* and sometimes *tyâjya*—the time to be avoided. And abandoning carefully all these evil hours the wealthy Brâhmiṇ built his mansion in ten years. The first entrance into a new house to dwell is performed always with a great deal of pomp and ceremony, even by the poor according to their means. And our wealthy Brâhmiṇ to please the gods of the other world and the gods of this world—*bhûsuras* Brâhmiṇs—spent a great deal of his wealth, and with *veoras* and music sounding all around him he entered into his house.

The whole of the day almost was spent in ceremonies and festivities. All the guests left the place at evening, and much exhausted by the exertions of the day the Brâhmiṇ house-owner retired to rest. Before sleep could close his eyelids he heard a fearful voice over his head exclaiming:—"Shall I fall down? Shall I fall down?"

Great was the concern of the landlord at hearing this voice. He thought that some demon had taken possession of his house, and that he was going to pull down the roof of his house over his own head. That very night with as much haste as he entered the new house, he vacated it and went back to his old house.

*Sirukakhaṭṭi perukavâḷka* is the Tamil proverb. The meaning of it is "build small and live great," *i.e.*, build small houses without laying out much capital uselessly in houses and live prosperously; and in villages many a rich landlord would prefer small houses to big ones. The idea that he had spent a great deal of money to build a big house troubled our hero. The spaciousness of the house was one reason for the devil to come in so easily, as he thought. When he vacated his house on the very night of the day he entered it people began to talk all sorts of scandals about it. The ladies in the bathing places (*ghaṭs*) in rivers began to give all sorts of colour to the devils in that house. One said that when she was coming to the river she saw a company of devils dancing round and round the middle pillar of the upper storey of that unfortunate house. Another said that she observed unearthly lights in that mansion the previous night. Thus people talked and talked, furnishing new colours and new adventures out of their pure imagination for a phenomena which they never saw. And our unfortunate rich man had to lock up his house which he built after so many days, and at the expense of so much money. Thus passed six months.

In that town there lived a poor beggar Brâhmiṇ. He was in extreme poverty, and spent a great portion of the day in begging from house to house his meal and clothes. He had, poor man, seven children. With this large family he was constantly in the greatest misery. He had not a proper house to live in. A miserable hut was all his wealth in that village. Winter was approaching, and the roof of their only hut began to fall down. The increasing miseries made the poor Brâhmiṇ resolve upon suicide. He could not bring himself to do that by his own hand. He had heard of the haunted house, and resolved to go there with all his family and perish by the hands of the devils. This was his secret intention, but he never spoke of it to any one. One day he came to the rich Brâhmiṇ who was the owner of the haunted mansion, and spoke to him thus:—

"My noble lord! The winter is approaching and the roof of my hut has fallen away. If you would kindly allow it I shall pass the rainy days in your big house."

When the rich man heard this he was very glad to see that one person at least there was in his little world who wanted the use of his house. So, without hesitating any longer, he replied:—

"My most holy sir, you can have the free use of that whole house for whatever time you may want it. It is enough if you light a lamp there and live happily. I built it, and I am not destined to live there. You can go and try your fortune there."

So said the rich landlord, and gave the key of that haunted house to the poor Brâhmiṇ. The latter took it, and with his family went and lived there from that day. That very night he also heard the same voice: "Shall I fall down?" "Shall I fall down?" twice. Nothing daunted, and quite resolved to perish with his wife and children, who were sound asleep near him, he exclaimed, "Fall down," and lo! a golden river of *mohurs* and *pagodas* began to fall down in the middle of the room from the top of the roof. It began falling and falling without any stopping till the poor Brâhmiṇ, who sat agape with wonder, began to fear that they would all be buried in *mohurs*. The moment he saw the sea of wealth before him, his idea of suicide abandoned him. "Stop please," said he at once, and the *mohur*-fall came to a sudden stop. He was delighted at the good nature of the devil, or whatever good spirit might have taken possession of the house, for its having given him so much wealth. He heaped up all the *mohurs* in one room, and locked it up, and had the key of it in his own possession. His wife and children got up during the *mohur*-fall. They also were informed of everything. The poor Brâhmiṇ advised his wife and children to keep the matter secret, and they, to their great credit, did so. They all—the poor parents and children—rejoiced at the good fortune that had made its visit to them.

As soon as morning dawned the poor Brâhmiṇ converted little by little his *mohurs* into money and bought grains and clothes for his family. This he did day by day till rumour began to spread that the poor Brâhmiṇ had found a treasure-trove in the rich landlord's house. Of course this rumour reached the ears of the wealthy man also. He came to the poor Brâhmiṇ and asked him all about the treasure-trove. The latter to his great honour related to the landlord every bit of the *mohur*-fall. He also wished to witness it and sleep in the room with the poor Brâhmiṇ, for the first time in his life, his thirst for *mohurs* inducing him to do so. At about midnight "Shall I fall down?" was again heard.

"Fall down" said the poor Brâhmiṇ, and lo! the *mohurs* began to descend like a water-fall. But, horror of horrors, they all appeared as so many scorpions to the house-owner. The poor man was heaping up thc gold coins, but all of them seemed to crawl as so many scorpions to the eyes of the landlord.

"Stop please," said the poor man, and the *mohur*-fall stopped.

Then turning to the house-owner, the poor man said: "My lord, you may take home this heap for your use."

The house-owner began to weep and said: "Most fortunate of mankind, I have heard my old father often repeat a proverb, 'To the fortunate fortune comes,' and its meaning I have discovered to-day only. I built the house and ran away when I heard the 'shall I fall.' No doubt I did very well, for had I remained a scorpion torrent would have sent me to the other world. Know then my most fortunate friend, that I see all your *mohurs* as so many scorpions. I have not the fortune to see them as *mohurs*. But you have that gift. So from this moment this house is yours. Whatever you can convert into money of your *mohurs* I shall receive and bless you."

So saying the house-owner came out of the room fearing the scorpions. And our poor man thus had all the fortune to himself, and was no longer a poor man. He soon became one of the wealthiest of men of his time, but remembering that he owed all his riches to the wealthy landlord who gave him the house, he used to share with the latter half of his wealth every year.

This story explains the Tamil proverb *Madrishṭam uḷḷavanukku kiḍaikkum;* to the fortunate good fortune.

N.B.—This story was also related to me by my step-mother whose birth-place is a village in the Trichinopoly district.

N. S.

# CHAPTER XXIV.

## RETALIATION—PALIKKUPPALI.

There is a proverb in Tamiḻ called *Palikkuppali vâṅgukiradu* which would best be translated by the expression "tit for tat," and the following story I heard when a boy from my step-mother, illustrating that proverb, and I have of late found the same story also in the Trichinopoly districts.

In a certain village there lived a poor Śûdra. He had made a vow to the goddess of his village, that if he came out successfully in a certain undertaking he would offer her a couple of goats. And he succeeded in his undertaking, and thought that his goddess alone had granted his request. Great was his joy and greater became his faith in her extraordinary powers. And as he promised he brought two fat goats and sacrificed them to her.

These goats thus sacrificed and the Śûdra sacrificer who meanwhile had died by a sudden fever, after a short time were all re-born in the world to undergo the results of their goodness or sin. The two goats, because they were sacrificed to the goddess, were re-born as the king and the minister of a large country. The Śûdra, as he had as much faith in his former life as in his goddess, was reborn in the priest's (*gurukkula*) caste, of course neither the king and his minister nor the priest had any reason to know their former life, until the death of the latter approached, as we shall presently see. A large kingdom fell to the share of the king, and he with his minister reigned over it most peacefully. In an unfrequented wilderness was a famous temple of a powerful goddess of of that country, and in that pagoda the priest regularly conducted her worship.

Thus passed several years, the king and minister happy in their own kingdom, and the priest executing his religious duties in the wilderness. The priest was leading a most calm and holy life, eating what grew in the wilderness. His life was as pure as pure can be.

But for all that fate would not forgive him for his acts in his former life.

The king and the minister had vowed to the goddess of the wilderness that if they returned successfully from the conquest of an enemy of theirs they would offer her some human sacrifice. And so they returned, and to make entire their vow to the goddess they left their kingdom like ordinary men and came to the wood. All along the way they searched for a person to sacrifice, but no one—fortunately for him—was to be found. They still thought that the vow must not be left unaccomplished, and resolved upon catching the priest of the temple and offering him up as their intended sacrifice. When such strong people like the king and his minister resolved to do so, what could the poor priest do? He was quite unable to escape when those two informed him of what they were going to do with him on his entering to worship the goddess. Said the priest:—

"Sirs! You have come here resolved upon offering me up as a sacrifice to the goddess. I cannot hereafter escape your hold. But if you would allow me to perform my *pûjâ* to the goddess this morning also, I shall gladly die after having done my duty."

So said the priest, and the king and the minister watched at the entrance and let him in.

The priest went into the *Garbhagṛiha*—the holy of the holies in the temple, and performed his worship to the goddess. After that was over he gave the image a severe blow on its back and thus addressed it:—

"Most merciless goddess. What have you done for all my faith in you. In this lonely wilderness, without knowing any other duty than your worship, I had been your true servant for the past many years. And in reward for all that, I must fall now a prey to the sacrifice of the king and the minister who are sharpening their knives outside to cut off my head at this moment. Is this the result of all my *pûjâ* (worship) to you."

So spake the priest, and the goddess, laughing, thus replied from the vacuum:—

"My true priest. Your acts in your former life must trouble you in this. And the charitable acts of this life, even, cannot protect you in your next birth. In your former birth you had murdered two goats. They were born as king and minister, and have dragged you here to murder you. But this—the murder you are to undergo soon, by these hands will relieve you only of one of the two murders of your former life. And for the other murder you and they would be re-born again, and again they would kill you. So in your next third life from this one you would enjoy the fruits of all this devotion. Since now you know the story of your former life, you will forgive me, I think."

Thus spoke the goddess, and the priest, as the knowledge of his former life dawned upon him, by the grace of the goddess, seemed resolved to die, in order to pay for his former sin. But the idea that in the next life he was to undergo the same punishment, vexed him much, and falling down at the goddess's feet, he respectfully requested her to try her best to let him off the next life; and the goddess's heart was also moved at the severity of fate which would make her devotee pass through one more life in misery before he enjoyed the fruits of his devotion. So she devised the following plan to exculpate him from his two crimes at the same time, and thus replied:—

"Priest! 'Intelligence can conquer even Fate,' is the proverb. When *Kâli* gave 500 years' life to Vikramâditya in his town, Bhatti, his minister, by making the king live six months in his capital and six months in the jungle, made his master's life to last for 1000 years. So by intelligence we conquer our fate too, sometimes. So hear my advice. Ask the king who has come to murder you to hold one end of the knife, and request his minister to hold the other end. Ask both of them to aim the blow at your neck; that will accomplish everything complete during this life. They will have no revenge to take from you in your next life."

So saying, the voice of the goddess stopped. The priest came back with a cheerful heart to the king and the minister, and asked them to oblige him by each of them holding one end of the knife and murdering him. They agreed, and performed thus their vow. The poor priest, too, without having another miserable life, was born a king in his next life, and lived in prosperity.

Here the story ends, and the story-teller in the Hindû household, and in my case my stepmother, would at once moralise, that if we did anything to any one in this life, that one would pay us out for it in our next life.

N.B.—I am led to think that this story does not contain a purely Hindû moral.

# CHAPTER XXV.

## THE BEGGAR AND THE FIVE MUFFINS.

In a certain village there lived a poor beggar and his wife. The man used to go out every morning with a clean vessel in his hand, return home with rice enough for the day's meal, and thus they lived on in extreme poverty.

One day a poor Mádhava Brâhmiṇ invited the pair to a feast, and among Mádhavas muffins (*tôśai*) are always a part of the good things on festive occasions. So during the feast the beggar and his wife had their fill of muffins. They were so pleased with them, that the woman was extremely anxious to prepare some muffins in her own house, and began to save a little rice every day from what her husband brought her for the purpose. When enough had been thus collected she begged a poor neighbour's wife to give her a little black pulse which the latter—praised be her charity—readily did. The faces of the beggar and his wife literally glowed with joy that day, for were they not to taste the long-desired muffins for a second time?

The woman soon turned the rice she had been saving, and the black pulse she had obtained from her neighbour into a paste, and mixing it well with a little salt, green chillies, coriander seed and curds, set it in a pan on the fire; and with her mouth watering all the while, prepared five muffins! By the time her husband had returned from his collection of alms, she was just turning out of the pan the fifth muffin! And when she placed the whole five muffins before him his mouth, too, began to water. He kept two for himself and two he placed before his wife, but what was to be done with the fifth? He did not understand the way out of this difficulty. That half and half made one, and that each could take two and a half muffins was a question too hard for him to solve. The beloved muffins must not be torn in pieces; so he said to his wife that either he or she must take the remaining one. But how were they to decide which should be the lucky one?

Proposed the husband:—"Let us both shut our eyes and stretch ourselves as if in sleep, each on a verandah on either side the kitchen. Whoever opens an eye and speaks first gets only two muffins; and the other gets three."

So great was the desire of each to get the three muffins, that they both abided by the agreement, and the woman, though her mouth watered for the muffins, resolved to go through the ordeal. She placed the five cakes in a pan and covered it over with another pan. She then carefully bolted the door inside and asking her husband to go into the east verandah, she lay down in the west one. Sleep she had none, and with closed eyes kept guard over her husband: for if he spoke first he would have only two muffins, and the other three would come to her share. Equally watchful was her husband over her.

Thus passed one whole day—two—three! The house was never opened! No beggar came to receive the morning dole. The whole village began to enquire after the missing beggar. What had become of him? What had become of his wife?

"See whether his house is locked on the outside and whether he has left us to go to some other village," spoke the greyheads.

So the village watchman came and tried to push the door open, but it would not open!

"Surely," said they, "it is locked on the inside! Some great calamity must have happened. Perhaps thieves have entered the house, and after plundering their property, murdered the inmates."

"But what property is a beggar likely to have?" thought the village assembly, and not liking to waste time in idle speculations, they sent two watchmen to climb the roof and open the latch from the inside.

Meanwhile the whole village, men, women, and children, stood outside the beggar's house to see what had taken place inside. The watchmen jumped into the house, and to their horror found the beggar and his wife stretched on opposite verandahs like two corpses. They opened the door, and the whole village rushed in. They, too, saw the beggar and his wife lying so still that they thought them to be dead. And though the beggar pair had heard everything that passed around them, neither would open an eye or speak. For whoever did it first would get only two muffins!

At the public expense of the village two green litters of bamboo and cocoanut leaves were prepared on which to remove the unfortunate pair to the cremation ground.

"How loving they must have been to have died together like this!" said some greybeards of the village.

In time the cremation ground was reached, and village watchmen had collected a score of dried cowdung cakes and a bundle of firewood from each house, for the funeral pyre. From these charitable contributions *two* pyres had been prepared, one for the man and one for the woman. The pyre was then lighted, and when the fire approached his leg, the man thought it time to give up the ordeal and to be satisfied with only two muffins! So while the villagers were still continuing the funeral rites, they suddenly heard a voice:—

"I shall be satisfied with two muffins!"

Immediately another voice replied from the woman's pyre:—

"I have gained the day; let me have the three!"

The villagers were amazed and ran away. One bold man alone stood face to face with the supposed dead husband and wife. He was a bold man, indeed for when a dead man or a man supposed to have died comes to life, village people consider him to be a ghost. However, this bold villager questioned the beggars until he came to know their story. He then went after the runaways and related to them the whole story of the five muffins to their great amazement.

But what was to be done to the people who had thus voluntarily faced death out of love for muffins. Persons who had ascended the green litter and slept on the funeral pyre could never come back to the village! If they did the whole village would perish. So the elders built a small hut in a deserted meadow outside the village and made the beggar and his wife live there.

Ever after that memorable day our hero and his wife were called the muffin beggar, and the muffin beggar's wife, and many old ladies and young children from the village use to bring them muffins in the morning and evening, out of pity for them, for had they not loved muffin so much that they underwent death in life?

# CHAPTER XXVI.

## THE BRAHMARÂKSHAS AND THE HAIR.

In a certain village there lived a very rich landlord, who owned several villages, but was such a great miser that no tenant would willingly cultivate his lands, and those he had gave him not a little trouble. He was indeed so vexed with them that he left all his lands untilled, and his tanks and irrigation channels dried up. All this, of course, made him poorer and poorer day by day. Nevertheless he never liked the idea of freely opening his purse to his tenants and obtaining their good will.

While he was in this frame of mind a learned *Sanyâsi* paid him a visit, and on his representing his case to him, he said:—

"My dear son,—I know an incantation (*mantra*) in which I can instruct you. If you repeat it for three months day and night, a Brahmarâkshas will appear before you on the first day of the fourth month. Make him your servant, and then you can set at naught all your petty troubles with your tenants. The Brahmarâkshas will obey all your orders, and you will find him equal to one hundred servants."

Our hero fell at his feet and begged to be instructed at once. The sage then sat facing the east and his disciple the landlord facing the west, and in this position formal instruction was given, after which the *Sanyâsi* went his way.

The landlord, mightily pleased at what he had learnt, went on practising the incantation, till, on the first day of the fourth month, the great Brahmarâkshas stood before him.

"What do you want, sir, from my hands?" said he; "what is the object of your having propitiated me for these three months?"

The landlord was thunderstruck at the huge monster who now stood before him and still more so at his terrible voice, but nevertheless he said:—

"I want you to become my servant and obey all my commands."

"Agreed," answered the Brahmarâkshas in a very mild tone, for it was his duty to leave off his impertinent ways when any one who had performed the required penance wanted him to become his servant; "Agreed. But you must always give me work to do; when one job is finished you must at once give me a second, and so on. If you fail I shall kill you."

The landlord, thinking that he would have work for several such Brahmarâkshasas, was pleased to see that his demoniacal servant was so eager to help him.

He at once took him to a big tank which had been dried up for several years, and pointing it out spoke as follows:—

"You see this big tank; you must make it as deep as the height of two palmyra trees and repair the embankment wherever it is broken."

"Yes, my master, your orders shall be obeyed," humbly replied the servant and fell to work.

The landlord, thinking that it would take several months, if not years, to do the work in the tank, for it was two *kos* long and one *kos* broad, returned delighted to his home, where his people were awaiting him with a sumptuous dinner. When enemies were approaching the Brahmarâkshas came to inform his master that he had finished his work in the tank. He was indeed astonished and feared for his own life!

"What! finished the work in one day which I thought would occupy him for months and years; if he goes on at this rate, how shall I keep him employed. And when I cannot find it for him he will kill me!" Thus he thought and began to weep; his wife wiped the tears that ran down his face, and said:—

"My dearest husband, you must not lose courage. Get out of the Brahmarâkshas all the work you can and then let me know. I'll give him something that will keep him engaged for a very very long time, and then he'll trouble us no more."

But her husband only thought her words to be meaningless and followed the Brahmarâkshas to see what he had done. Sure enough the thing was as complete as could be, so he asked him to plough *all* his lands, which extended over twenty villages! This was done in two *ghaṭikâs*! He next made him dig and cultivate *all* his garden lands. This was done in the twinkling of an eye! The landlord now grew hopeless.

"What more work have you for me?" roared the Brahmarâkshas, as he found that his master had nothing for him to do, and that the time for his eating him up was approaching.

"My dear friend," said he, "my wife says she has a little job to give you; do it please now. I think that that is the last thing I can give you to do, and after it in obedience to the conditions under which you took service with me, I must become your prey!"

At this moment his wife came to them, holding in her left hand a long hair, which she had just pulled out from her head, and said:—

"Well, Brahmarâkshas, I have only a very light job for you. Take this hair, and when you have made it straight, bring it back to me."

The Brahmarâkshas calmly took it, and sat in a *pîpal* tree to make it straight. He rolled it several times on his thigh and lifted it up to see if it became straight; but no, it would still bend! Just then it occurred to him that goldsmiths, when they want to make their metal wires straight, have them heated in fire; so he went to a fire and placed the hair over it, and of course it frizzled up with a nasty smell! He was horrified!

"What will my master's wife say if I do not produce the hair she gave me?"

So he became mightily afraid, and ran away.

This story is told to explain the modern custom of nailing a handful of hair to a tree in which devils are supposed to dwell, to drive them away.

# NOTES.

## NOTES TO XIII.—FIRST PART.

Few stories are more familiar and widely spread than that of the Lost Camel, which occurs in the opening of the romance. It was formerly, and perhaps is still, reproduced in English school reading-books. Voltaire, in chapter iii. of his "Zadig; ou, La Destinée" (the materials of which he is said to have derived from Geuelette's "Soirées Bretonnes,") has a version in which a lost palfrey and a she dog are ded scribed by the "sage" from the traces they had left on the path over which they passed. The great Arabian historian and traveller Mas'udi, in his "Meadows of Gold, and Mines of Gems," written A.D. 943, gives the story of the Lost Camel, and from Mas'udi it was probably taken into the MS. text of the "Thousand and One Nights," procured in the East (?Constantinople) by Wortley Montague, and now preserved in the Bodleian Library, Oxford.[102] In that MS. it forms an incident in the story of the Sultan of Yeman and his Three Sons: the princes, after their father's death, quarrel over the succession to the throne, and at length agree to lay their respective claims before one of the tributary princes. On the road one of them remarks, "A camel has lately passed this way loaded with grain on one side, and with sweetmeats on the other." The second observes, "and the camel is blind of one eye." The third adds, "and it has lost its tail." The owner comes up, and on hearing their description of his beast, forces them to go before the king of the country, to whom they explain how they discovered the defects of the camel and its lading. In a Persian work, entitled "Nigaristan," three brothers rightly conjecture in like manner that a camel which had passed, and which they had not seen, was blind of an eye, wanted a tooth, was lame, and laden with oil on the one side, and honey on the other. The story is also found in the Hebrew Talmud. Two slaves are overheard by their master conversing about a camel that had gone before them along the road. It was blind of an eye, and laden with two skin bottles, one of which contained wine, the other oil. In a Siberian version (Radloff), three youths are met by a man who asks them if they had seen his camel, to which they reply by describing the colour and defects of the animal so exactly that he accuses them to the Prince of having stolen it. "I have lost a camel, my lord," said he, "and when I met these three young men we saluted, and I told them that I had lost my camel. Quoth one of these youths, 'Was thy camel of a light colour?' The second asked, 'was thy camel lame?' And the third, 'Was it not blind of an eye?' I answered Yes to their questions. Now decide, my lord. It is evident these young men have stolen

[102] It is not generally known that the "Birnam Wood" incident in Shakespeare's "Macbeth" occurs in the same Arabian historical work.

my camel." Then the Prince asked the eldest, "How did you know that the camel was of a light colour?" He replied, "By some hairs which has fallen on the ground when it had rubbed itself against trees." The two others gave answers similar to those in our version. Then said the Prince to the man, "Thy camel is lost; go and look for it." So the stranger mounted his horse and departed.

## NOTES TO XIII.—THE SECOND PART.

*The Hunter and his Faithful Dog.*—A variety of this story is cited from a Cawnpore newspaper, in the "Asiatic Journal," Vol. XV. (new series), Part II. October, 1834, p. 78, which is to the following effect:—A Bunjarrah named Dabee had a dog called Bhyro, the faithful companion of his travels, who guarded his goods from robbers while he slept. He wished to go to a distant part of the country to trade in grain, but had not sufficient funds for the purpose. After much cogitation, he at length resolved to pledge his dog for 1,000 rupees, and when he applied to several persons was laughed at for his folly; but a wealthy merchant named Dyaram gave the money, on condition that it should be paid back within twelve months, taking the dog Bhyro in pledge. When eleven months had passed, the merchant began to bewail the stupidity which had induced him to lend so large a sum on so precarious a security. His relentings were, however, premature. One dark and dreary night he was aroused from his slumbers by a great noise, occasioned by the clashing of swords and the barking of Bhyro. A band of armed men had entered the house with intent to plunder, but before they could effect their purpose they had been observed by the faithful Bhyro, who commenced an attack upon them. Before Dyaram could render any assistance, Bhyro had laid two of the robbers dead at his feet; a third, on the approach of Dyaram, aimed a blow at his head, which was prevented from taking effect by Bhyro seizing the ruffian by the throat and laying him prostrate on the ground. After peace was restored, Dyaram congratulated himself on having received Bhyro in pledge for the Bunjarrah, by which act he not only escaped being plundered, but in all probably murdered. Next morning Dyaram called Bhyro, and after caressing him, said:—"The service you rendered me last night is more than an equivalent for the 1,000 rupees I lent your master; go, faithful creature. I give you a free discharge from your obligation as security for him." Bhyro shook his head in token that it was impossible for him to go until his master returned; but Dyaram, comprehending his meaning, soon arranged matters by writing a statement of the circumstances, and giving a voucher for the 1,000 rupees. This document he tied round Bhyro's neck, which done, Bhyro expressed his delight by leaping about in every direction, and, after licking the hands of Dyaram, darted out of the house and set off in quest of his master. While these scenes were transpiring in Dyaram's house, Dabee was not unmindful of the pledge he had left behind him, and, having succeeded in his speculation, was returning with all haste to redeem it. At his last stage homewards he was surprised to see Bhyro approaching him with every demonstration of joy, but at sight of him Dabee's rage was kindled, and repulsing Bhyro as he fawned upon him he thus addressed him:—"O, ungrateful wretch! is this the return you have made for my kindness to you? and is this the manner in which you have established my character for veracity? You remained faithful to your trust during eleven months—could you not have held out for thirty short days? You have, by your desertion from your post, entailed dishonour upon me, and for this you shall die." And, so saying, he drew his sword and slew him. After having committed this deed, he observed a paper tied round Bhyro's neck; having read it, his grief was indescribable. To atone in some measure for his rash act, caused poor Bhyro to be buried on the spot where he fell, and a superb monument to be erected over his remains. To the grave of Bhyro, even at the present day, resort natives who have been bitten by dogs, they believing that the dust collected there, when applied to the wounds, is an antidote for hydrophobia.

## NOTES TO XIII.—THE THIRD PART.

*The Brahman's Wife and the Mongoose.*—We have, in this story, an Indian variety of the well-known Welsh legend of Llewellyn and his dog Gellert. A similar legend was current in France during the Middle Ages. But our story—*mutatis mutandis*—is as old as the third century B.C., since it is found in a Buddhist work of that period. It also occurs in two Sanskrit forms of the celebrated Fables of Pilpay, or Bidnaia namely the "Pancha Tantra" (five chapters), which is said to date as far back as the 5th century A.D., and the "Hitopadesa" (Friendly Counsels); also in the Arabian and other Eastern versions of the same work. It is found in all the texts of the Book of Sindibad—Greek, Syriac, Persian, Hebrew, Old Castilian, Arabic, &c., and in the several European versions, known generally under the title of "The History of the Seven Wise Masters," the earliest form of which being a Latin prose work entitled "Dolopathos." There are, of course, differences in the details of the numerous versions both Western and Eastern, but the fundamental outline is the same in all. In my work on the migrations of popular tales, I have reproduced all the known versions of this world-wide story, with the exception of that in the present romance, which is singular in representing the woman as killing herself after she had discovered her fatal mistake, and her husband as slaying his little son and himself. The author of the romance probably added these tragedies, in order to enable the supposed narrator to more forcibly impress the king with the grievous consequences of acting in affairs of moment with inconsiderateness and precipitation. In most versions it is the husband who kills the faithful animal. Among the Malays the story of the Snake and the Mongoose is current in this form:—A man left a tame bear in charge of his house, and of his sleeping child, while he was absent from home. On his return he missed his child, the house was in disorder, as if some great struggle had taken place, and the floor was covered with blood. Hastily concluding that the bear had killed and devoured the child, the enraged father slew the animal with his spear, but almost immediately afterwards found the carcase of a tiger, which the faithful bear had defeated and killed, and the child emerged unharmed from the jungle, where it had taken refuge.

In a black-letter English edition of the "Seven Wise Masters," the knight, having slain his hound and discovered his child safe in its cradle, exclaims (and here the hand of the misogynist monkish writer is very evident!)—"Woe be to me, that, for the words of my wife, I have slain my good and best greyhound, the which had saved my child's life, and hath slain the serpent; therefore I will put myself to penance." And so he brake his sword in three pieces, and travelled in the direction of the Holy Land, and abode there all the days of his life. The preceding story of the Hunter and his Dog, it will be observed, is closely allied to that of the Brahman's Wife and the Mongoose; and in conclusion, where the hunter erects a stately tomb over his dog's remains, it presents a striking resemblance to the Welsh legend of Llewellyn and the dog Gellert, which is probably not merely fortuitous.

A very curious version is found in a black-letter chapter-book, entitled the "Seven Wise Mistresses," written in imitation of the "Seven Wise Masters," by one Thomas Howard, about the end of the seventeenth century, in which a knight and his lady are wrecked and cast ashore on a desert island, and the knight soon afterwards dies. His wife takes a thorn out of a lion's foot (Androcles in petticoats), and the grateful animal follows her about, and provides her with food, and this is how the story goes on:—

"At last she began mourning to herself, deploring her condition in living in such obscurity in a foreign Country, and as her daily companion, a savage Beast, her mind yearning after her own habitation, she thus complained: 'Oh, how hath fortune frowned on me that I am driven out from all human knowledge, and am glad to take up my habitation with the Beast of the Field!'

"As she thus complained to herself, the Devil chanced to appear to her, and demanded the cause of her complaint, and she related all to him as you have heard. Then said he to her: 'What wilt thou give and I will provide a ship which shall carry thee home to thy own country.' She answered: 'Half my Estates.'

"'Nay,' said the Devil, 'If thou wilt give me thy Soul at the term of twelve years, I will set thee down in thy own country, and thou shalt live and flourish so long.' 'God forbid,' said the Lady. 'I would rather end my wretched life in this solitary island than that.' 'Why then,' said the Devil, 'I will make this bargain with you, that if you abstain from sleeping all the time of our voyage, which shall be but three days, I will have nothing to do with your Soul; if you sleep, I will have it as I have said.'

"And upon this bargain the lady ventured, provided she might have her Lion with her. So 'twas concluded, and a brave Ship came and took the Lady and her Lion. When she lay down the Lion lay by her, and if she slumbered the Lion would touch her with his paw, by which means he kept her awake all the voyage, until she landed in her own country, and being come to her Father's house, she knocked at the gate. Then the Porter coming with all speed opened the gate and thought that it was a Beggar.

"Frowningly he shut it again, saying, 'There's nothing here for you.' Then she bounced at the gate again, and asked the Porter if such a Knight lived there, meaning her Father, and he said 'Yes.' 'Then,' said she, 'Pray, deliver this piece of ring unto him.' Now this ring was it she brake betwixt her Father and she at her departure out of the land. Then the Porter delivered the Ring to his Master, saying: 'The Beggar woman at the gate willed me to deliver the piece of ring unto you.'

"When the Knight saw the ring he fell down in a swound but when he was revived he said, 'Call her in, for she is my only Daughter, whom I thought was dead.' 'Then,' said the Porter, 'I dare not call her in, for there is a mighty Lion with her.' 'Though it be,' said the Knight, 'call her in.' Then said the Porter [to the Lady], 'You are to come in, but leave your Lion outside.' 'No,' said the Lady, 'my Lion goes whereever I go, and where he is not, there will I not be.'

"And when she came to her Father she fell down on her knees and wept. Her Father took her up in his arms and kissed her, weeping as fast, and after he clothed her in purple, and placed her by him in a chair, and demanded an account of her travels, and she told him all that had happened, and how the Lion had saved her life, and was the greatest comfort she had in the Wilderness. It chanced afterwards that as the Knight was going into his Wood to look after his young Horses, he met with a wild Boar, with whom he fell in combat. The Lion loved the Old Knight, and by accident walking along he scented the Boar, and as the Lion ran toward the place where the Boar was, the Steward espied him, and he ran into the Palace, and cryed out, 'the Lion is running after my Master to destroy him.'

"Then the Lady sent after him ten of her servants, who met the Lion, his mouth all bloody, and they ran back and told the Lady the Lion had destroyed her aged Father. Then said the Lady, 'O woe is me that ever I was born, that have brought a Lion from far to destroy my own Father.' Therefore she commanded her servants to slay the Lion, which no sooner was done but her Father came in, and said; 'O, I have met with a wild Boar, with whom I fought, and there came the Lion to my aid, and slew the Boar, and so saved my life, else I had died by the Boar.'

"When the Lady heard this, O how she wept and wrung her hands, saying, 'For the words of a wicked Steward, I have slain my good Lion, who hath saved my life and my Father's. Cursed be the time I was advised by him.'"

*The Faithless Wife and the Ungrateful Blind Man.*—I do not remember having met with this story in any other collection, although there are there many tales in Asiatic story-books of women abandoning their blind or infirm husbands, and going off with strange men. A very considerable proportion, in fact of Eastern stories turn upon the alleged wickedness and profligacy and intrigues of women. This most unjust estimate of "the sex" seems to have been universal in Asiatic countries from every remote times and probably was introduced into Europe through the Crusades. Not a few of the mediæval Monkish tales represent women in a very unfavourable light, and this is also the case in our early English jest-books, which were compiled soon after the invention of printing. In the oldest Indian literature, however, especially the two grand epics "Ramayana" and "Mahabharata," occur several notable tales of noble women, such as "Dushyanta and Sakuntala," and the charming romance of "Nala and Damayanti;" and in another work, the "Adventures of the Ten princes," ("Dasa Kumara Charita,") the fine story of Gomiui, who is held up as a pattern to her sex.

## NOTES TO XIII.—THE FOURTH PART.

*The Wonderful Mango-fruit.*—A variety of this story occurs in the Persian "Tuti Nama" of Nakhshabi:—A Prince, who is very ill, sends a parrot of great sagacity to procure him some fruit of the Tree of Life. When at length the bird returns with the life-giving fruit, the Prince scruples to eat of it, upon which the parrot relates the legend of "Solomon and the Water of Immortality;" how that wise monarch declined to procure immunity from death, on consideration that he should thus survive all his friends and female favourites. The Prince, however, being suspicious regarding the fruit, sent some trusty messengers to "bring the first apple that fell from the Tree of Existence." But it happened that a black snake had poisoned it by seizing it in its mouth and then letting it drop again. When the messengers returned with the fruit, the Prince tried the effect on a holy man, who instantly falls down dead. Upon seeing this, the Prince dooms the parrot to death; but the sagacious bird suggests that, before the Prince should execute him for treason, he should himself go to the Tree of Life and make another experiment with its fruit. The Prince does so, and, returning home, gives part of the fruit to an old woman, "who, from age and infirmity, had not stirred abroad for many years;" and, no sooner had she tasted it, than she was changed into a charming girl of eighteen. But more closely resembling our story is a version in a Canarese collection, entitled "Katha Manjari":—A certain king had a magpie that flew one day to heaven with another magpie. From thence it took away some mango seed, and, having returned, gave it to the king, saying:—

"If you cause this to be planted and grow, whoever eats of its fruit old age will forsake him and his youth be restored."

The king was much pleased, and caused it to be planted in his favourite garden. After some years, buds appeared and became flowers, then young fruit, then full grown; and when the fruit was ripe the king ordered one to be plucked and brought to him, when he gave it to an old man. But on it had fallen poison from a serpent as it was carried through the air by a kite, so the old man immediately withered and died. The king, on seeing this, exclaimed in wrath:—

"Is not this bird attempting to kill me?" And he seized the magpie and wrung off its head. Afterwards in the village the tree had the name of the poisonous mango. Now, it happened that a washerman, taking the part of his wife in a quarrel with his old mother, struck the latter, who was so angry at her son that she resolved to die, in order that the blame of her death should fall upon him; and having gone to the poisonous mango-tree in the garden, she cut off a fruit and ate it, when instantly she became more blooming than a girl of sixteen. This miracle she published everywhere and it came to the king's ears, who, having called her and seen her, caused the fruit to be given to other old people. Having seen what was thus done by the marvelous virtue of the mango-fruit, the king sorrowfully exclaimed:—

"Alas, the faithful magpie is killed which gave me this divine tree! How guilty am I!" And he pierced himself with his sword and died.

"Therefore," adds the story-teller, "those who act without thought are certain to be ruined." The old Brahman's generously presenting the king with the wonderful mango-fruit in our story, finds its parallel with a difference, in the Hindu romance entitled "Simhasana Dwatrinsatri," or Thirty-two Tales of a throne, where a Brahman having received from the gods, as a reward for his devotional austerities, the fruit of immortality, joyfully proceeds home and shows it to his wife, who advises him to give it to the Raja Bhartrihari, as the wealth he should receive in return were preferable to an endless life of poverty. He goes to the palace, and presenting the fruit to the Raja, acquaints him of its nature, and is rewarded with a lakh of rupees. The Raja gives the fruit to his wife, telling her that if she ate it her beauty would increase day by day, and she should be immortal. The Kani gives it to her paramour, the chief of police, who, in his turn, presents it as the choicest of gifts to a courtesan, who, after reflecting that it would only enable her to commit innumerable sins, resolves to offer it to the Raja, in hope of a reward in a future life. When Raja Bhartrihari receives the fruit again he is astonished, and, on learning from the *hætera* from whom she had obtained it, he knew that his queen was unfaithful, and, abandoning his throne and kingdom, departs into the jungle, where he became an ascetic.

## NOTES TO XIII.—THE FIFTH PART.

*The Poisoned Food.*—This is a third instance of food or fruit being poisoned by serpents, and it occurs very frequently in Eastern stories. The oldest form of this tale is found in a Sanskrit collection entitled "Twenty-five Tales of a Vampyre" (*Vetalapanchavimsati*), which is probably of Buddhist extraction, and which also exists in many of the vernacular languages of India. The wife of a man named Harisvamin having been stolen from him one night by a Vidyadhara Prince, he gave away all his wealth to the Brahmans, and resolved to visit the sacred waters to wash away his sins, after which he hoped to recover his beloved wife; and the story thus proceeds:—Then he left the country, with his Brahman birth as his only fortune, and began to go round to all the sacred bathing-places in order to recover his beloved. And as he was roaming about there came upon him the terrible lion of the hot season, with the blazing sun for mouth and with a mane composed of his fiery rays. And the winds blew with excessive heat, as if warmed by the breath of sighs furnaced forth by travellers grieved at being separated from their wives. And the tanks, with their supply of water diminished by the heat and their drying white mud, appeared to be showing their broken hearts. And the trees by the roadside seemed to lament on account of the departure of the glory of spring, making their wailing heard in the shrill moaning of their bark, with leaves, as it were, lips, parched with heat.

At that season Harisvamin, wearied out with the heat of the sun, with bereavement, hunger and thirst, and continual travelling, emaciated and dirty, and pining for food, reached in the course of his wanderings a certain village, and found in it the house of a Brahman named Padmanabha, who was engaged in a sacrifice. And, seeing that many Brahmans were eating in his house, he stood leaning against the door-post, silent and motionless. And the good wife of that Brahman named Padmanabha, seeing him in this position, felt pity for him, and reflected:—

"Alas! mighty is hunger! Whom will it not bring down? For here stands a man at the door, who appears to be a householder, desiring food, with downcast countenance; evidently come from a long journey, and with all his faculties impaired by hunger. So is not he a man to whom food ought to be given?" Having gone through these reflections, that kind woman took up in her hand a vessel full of rice boiled in milk, with *ghî* and sugar, and brought it, and courteously presented it to him, and said:—

"Go and eat this somewhere on the bank of the lake, for this place is unfit to eat in, as it is filled with feasting Brahmans." He said "I will do so," and took the vessel of rice and placed it at no great distance under a banyan-tree on the edge of the lake; and he washed his hands and feet in the lake, and rinsed his mouth, and then came back in high spirits to eat the rice. But while he was thus engaged a kite, holding a black cobra with its beak and claws, came and sat on that tree. And it so happened that poisonous saliva issued from the mouth of that dead snake, which the bird had captured and was carrying along. The saliva fell into the dish of rice which was placed under the tree, and Harisvamin, without observing it, came and ate up that rice. As soon as in his hunger he had devoured all that food, he began to suffer terrible agonies, caused by the poison. He exclaimed:—

"When fate has turned against a man, everything in this world turns also; accordingly this rice has become poison to me." Thus speaking, Harisvamin, tortured with the poison, tottered to the house of that Brahman who was engaged in a sacrifice, and said to his wife:—

"The rice which you gave me has poisoned me; so fetch me quickly a charmer who can counteract the operation of poison; otherwise you will be guilty of the death of a Brahman." When Harisvamin had said this to the good woman, who was beside herself to think what it could all mean, his eyes closed and he died.

Then the Brahman who was engaged in a sacrifice drove his wife out of the house, though she was innocent and hospitable, being enraged with her for the supposed murder of her guest. The good woman, for her part, having incurred groundless blame from her charitable deed, and so become burdened with infamy, went to a holy bathing-place, to perform penance. Then there was a discussion before the superintendent of religion as to which of the four parties, the kite, the snake, and the couple who gave rice, was guilty of the murder of a Brahman; but the question was not decided.

It will be seen that our story differs very considerably from the foregoing, which we must regard as the original. The same story occurs in all the Eastern versions of the Book of Sindibad, but in most of these it is not a traveller who is thus poisoned, but a wealthy man and his guests; having sent a domestic to the market to buy sour curds, which she carried back in an open vessel, poison from a serpent in a stork's mouth dropped into the curds, of which the master of the house and his guests partook and died. The story is probably more than 2,000 years old.

*"Eating up the Protector."*—Akin to this, but with a very different conclusion, is the well-known story of the traveller who released a tiger from a trap into which he had fallen. The Brahman's fidelity to his pact with the serpent reminds one of the Arabian story of the Merchant and the Genie. In a Tamil tale, a cow having given herself up to a tiger to redeem her owner (it is to be understood, of course, that both animals are human beings re-born in those forms) she obtains leave to go

and suckle her calf, after which she returns when the tiger, moved by her fidelity, lets her go free.

The serpent's emitting gems recalls Shakespeare's allusion to the popular notion of the "toad, ugly and venomous, which bears a precious jewel in its head." It is a very ancient and widespread belief that serpents are the guardians of hidden treasures. Preller, in his work on Grecian mythology, refers to a Servian story in which a shepherd, as in our tale, saves the life of a snake in a forest fire, and, in return for this service, the snake's father gives him endless treasures and teaches him the language of birds. There is a very similar story in Dozon's "Contes Albanais."

In the charming tale of "Nala and Damayanti," which occurs in the third part ("Vana Parva") of the grand Indian epic "Mahabharata," the exiled king perceives a snake with a ray of jewels in its crest, writhing in a jungle fire, and lifting it out, carries it some distance, and is about to set it down, when the snake says to him, "Carry me ten steps farther, and count them aloud as you go." So Nala proceeds, counting the steps—one, two, three—and when he said "ten" (*dasa,* which means "ten" and also "bite") the snake took him at his word, and bit the king in the forehead, upon which he became black and deformed.

An abstract of a considerably modified form of our romance orally current among the people of Bengal may be given in conclusion: A king appoints his three sons to patrol in turn the streets of his capital during the night. It happens that the youngest Prince in going his rounds one night sees a beautiful woman issuing from the royal palace, and accosting her, asks her business at such an hour. She replies:—

"I am the guardian deity of this palace; the king will be killed this night, therefore I am going away."

The Prince persuades the goddess to return into the palace and await the event. As in our story, he enters his father's sleeping chamber and discovers a huge cobra near the royal couch. He cuts the serpent into many pieces, which he puts inside a brass vessel that is in the room. Then seeing that some drops of the serpent's blood had fallen on his step-mother's breast, he wraps a piece of cloth round his tongue to protect it from the poison, and licks off the blood. The lady awakes, and recognises him as he is leaving the room. She accuses him to the king of having used an unpardonable freedom with her. In the morning the king sends for his eldest son, and asks him: "If a trusted servant should prove faithless how should he be punished?"

Quoth the Prince: "Surely his head should be parted from his body; but before doing so you should ascertain whether the man is actually guilty."

And then he proceeds to relate the following story:—"Once upon a time there was a goldsmith who had a grown-up son, whose wife was acquainted with the language of animals, but she kept secret from her husband and all others the fact of her being endowed with such a rare gift. It happened one night she heard a jackal exclaim: 'There is a dead body floating on the river; would that some one might give me that body to eat, and for his pains take the diamond ring from the finger of the dead man.'

"The woman arose from her bed and went to the bank of the river, and her husband, who was not asleep, followed her unobserved. She went into the water, drew the corpse to land, and unable to loosen the ring from the dead man's finger, which had swelled, she bit off the finger, and leaving the corpse on the bank, returned home, whither she had been preceded by her husband. Almost petrified with fear, the young goldsmith concluded from what he had seen that his wife was not a human being, but a ghoul (*rakshasi*), and early in the morning he hastened to his father and related the whole affair to him—how the woman had got up during the night and gone to the river, out of which she dragged a dead body to the land, and was busy devouring it when he ran home in horror.

"The old man was greatly shocked, and advised his son to take his wife on some pretext into the forest and leave her there to be destroyed by wild beasts. So the husband caused the woman to get herself ready to go on a visit to her father, and after a hasty breakfast they set out. In going through a dense jungle, where the goldsmith proposed abandoning his wife, she heard a serpent cry, 'O, passenger, I pray thee to seize and give me that croaking frog, and take for thy reward the gold and precious stones concealed in yonder hole.' The woman at once seized the frog and threw it towards the serpent, and then began digging into the ground with a stick. Her husband quaked with fear, thinking that his ghoul-wife was about to kill him, but she called to him, saying, 'My dear husband, gather up all this gold and precious gems.'

"Approaching the spot with hesitation he was surprised to perceive an immense treasure laid bare by his wife, who then explained to him how she had learned of it from the snake that lay coiled up near them, whose language she understood. Then he said to his wife—'It is now so late that we cannot reach your father's house before dark, and we might be slain by wild beasts. Let us therefore return home.' So they retraced their steps, and approaching the house the goldsmith said to his wife—'Do, you, my dear, go in by the back door, while I enter by the front and show my father all this treasure.'

The woman went in by the back door and was met by her father-in-law, who, on seeing her, concluded that she had killed and devoured his son, and striking her on the head with a hammer which he happened to have in his hand, she instantly expired. Just then the son came into the room, but it was too late."

"I have told your Majesty this story," adds the eldest Prince, "in order that before putting the man to death you should make sure that he is guilty."

The king next calls his second son and asks him the same question, to which he replies by relating a story to caution his father against rash actions.

"A king, separated from his attendants while engaged in the chase, saw what he conceived to be rain-water dropping from the top of a tree, and, being very thirst, held his drinking cup under it until it was nearly filled, and, just as he was about to put it to his lips, his horse purposely moved so as to cause the contents to be spilled on the ground, upon which the king in a rage drew his sword and killed the faithful animal; but afterwards discovering that what he had taken for rain-water was poison that dropped from a cobra in the tree, his grief knew no bounds."

Calling lastly his third son, the king asks him what should be done to the man who proved false to his trust. The Prince tells the story of the wonderful tree, the fruit of which bestowed on him who ate of it perennial youth, with unimportant variations from the version in our romance.

Then the Prince explained the occasion of his presence in the Royal bedchamber, and how he had saved the king and his consort from the cobra's deadly bite. And the king, overjoyed and full of gratitude, strained his faithful son to his heart, and ever after cherished and loved him with all a father's love.

9 789356 148123

Printed by Libri Plureos GmbH in Hamburg,
Germany